MY STORY
JOANNE HAYES

BRANDON

First published 1985
Brandon Book Publishers Ltd.
Dingle, Co. Kerry, Ireland
and 51 Washington Street
Dover, New Hampshire 03820, U.S.A.

© Joanne Hayes and John Barrett 1985.

All rights reserved. No part of this publication may be reproduced, stored in a retrieval system, or transmitted, in any form or by any means, electronic, mechanical, photocopying, recording, or otherwise, without the prior permission of Brandon Book Publishers.

Cover photos: Derek Speirs/Report
Cover design: Steven Hope
Typesetting: Printset & Design Ltd., Dublin
Printed and bound in the Republic of Ireland

To Yvonne

Yvonne and Joanne. (Michael MacSweeney).

Contents

Preface 8
Introduction 10
Who's on Trial? 20
The Good Life 22
Jeremiah 31
Alone in a Field 37
Interrogation 43
In Prison, Hospital and the Courts ... 49
The Tribunal Starts 63
Giving Evidence 80
An Immovable Force 126
Experts 142
John Courtney 153
Final Stages 158
Judge Lynch Reports 171
Appendix: The Statements 180

List of Illustrations

Yvonne and Joanne 5
Nell McCafferty, John Barrett and Willie Leahy 19
Women demonstrate 21
Mary and Paddy Hayes, Joanne, Kathleen, Mike and Ned 23
Maurice Fuller 23

Ned, Joanne and Mike   23
Bridie Fuller, Mary Hayes, Mike, Ned, Joanne
and Kathleen   26
Joanne's First Communion   26
Yvonne, Ned, Joanne, Mary, Kathleen and Mike   26
Jeremiah Locke   30
Joanne and Yvonne at home   33
Detective Superintendent John Courtney   42
Slea Head   48
P.J. Browne and Gerry O'Carroll   48
Martin Kennedy   64
Judge Lynch   64
Brian Curtin, Patrick Mann and Dermot McCarthy   64
Martina Ronan, Mary O'Riordan and Joanne   69
Demonstration on 23 January   100
Escort through the women's demonstration   100
On the farm   108
Reading letters of support   170

Glossary

Ban Gharda	policewoman
Ceann Comhairle	chairperson of the Dail
Dail	lower house of parliament
Fianna Fail	largest political party in the Republic of Ireland
Fine Gael	second largest political party, in government in coalition with the Labour Party at the time of the Tribunal
Garda	policeman
Gardai	police
Garda Siochana	police force of the Republic of Ireland
Oireachtas	parliament
Seanad	second chamber of parliament
TD (Teachta Dala)	member of the Dail

Preface

I WATCH YVONNE POTTERING around the kitchen playing with her toys and running to one of us for help whenever something goes wrong. At these moments I envy her her innocence and remind myself that I too was happy and carefree once and that this kitchen used to be my playroom.

In the years to come I will have a complex and harrowing story to tell her of love and tears, joy and heartache and immense suffering, and I can only pray that when she has heard that story the bond between us will be strong enough to help her understand, and love and respect me as much as I love her.

Through the terrible months since 1 May 1984 my life has become public property and my body a subject for discussion all over the world. The Tribunal saw to that. Set up to inquire into the questioning, charging and subsequent dropping of charges against me and my family, the Tribunal developed into an ordeal for which we were never prepared and which we will never forget. We were offered as a family for public discussion in a manner unprecedented in this country.

During those months we received considerable public support, for which we are sincerely grateful. Inevitably there was criticism too, much of which we never heard about; but, at any rate, the media coverage and callous invasion of our privacy enabled people to make up their own minds about us. Sadly, the issues that were involved tended to get overlooked along the way.

I do not plead for sympathy now, nor seek to justify my actions, and most of all I want to avoid causing any further hurt to innocent victims of my behaviour. I acted recklessly and selfishly and I am deeply sorry for all the trouble that I have caused for so many people.

But the past cannot be changed, the hurts cannot be easily healed, and for me the future must belong to Yvonne for she is my life now, my reason to live. Without her I wouldn't have got through this. At the darkest times I'd think of her — that's what's kept me going.

Others will write their versions of what became known as the

"Kerry Babies" case. They will make judgements and offer opinions. What follows here is my story, the unvarnished account that will not attempt to solve the mystery of the Caherciveen baby but will, I hope, answer some of the questions about me and my family that even the lawyers never asked.

                        Joanne Hayes,
                        Abbeydorney, Co. Kerry.
                        October 1985.

Don't Quit

When things go wrong, as they sometimes will,
When the road you're trudging seems all uphill,
When funds are low and the debts are high,
And you want to smile, but you have to sigh,
When care is pressing you down a bit,
Rest if you must, but don't you quit.

Life is queer with its twists and turns,
As every one of us sometimes learns,
And many a person turns about
When they might have won had they stuck it out.
Don't give up though the pace seems slow,
You may succeed with another blow.

Often the struggler has given up
When he might have captured the victor's cup;
And he learned too late when the night came down,
How close he was to the golden crown.

Success is failure turned inside out
So stick to the fight when you're hardest hit,
It's when things seem worst that you mustn't quit.

   I owe a lot to that poem, and to the person who sent it to me. I read the poem many times and found the resilience to resume the uneven contest. Otherwise the fact that I was telling the truth might not have been enough to sustain me.

   "Don't Quit" is published by Family Life Centre, Knock.

Introduction

ON SATURDAY 14 APRIL 1984 at about 8.30 in the evening John (Jack) Griffin, a farmer of Kimego, Caherciveen, was jogging along a grassy edge of the White Strand near his home on the beautiful and rugged South Kerry coast. He was going to check on his cattle which were grazing in a field on the other side of the beach. As he ran his attention was drawn to a plastic fertiliser bag on the rocks below him. Beside it he saw what he at first thought was a naked, black-haired doll lying wedged face downwards between two rocks.

John Griffin had stumbled on what was to become known as the Caherciveen baby, the first casualty in a sad and morbid series of events that would eventually reverberate through the top ranks of the country's police force. It would also initiate an ordeal of unprecedented dimensions for a family who lived more than fifty miles away in the fertile farmland of North Kerry.

John Griffin ran two miles to the home of a friend and asked Brendan O'Shea, an apprentice electrician who was visiting the house, to drive him back to the White Strand. The men inspected the gruesome find more closely now and discovered that it was a male infant and was cold to touch. The body looked white and "plasticy", they said later. The Gouldings 0-7-30 fertiliser bag had been tied with string, but was torn and they saw another brown bag inside it.

The tide was out so the men left a marker at the scene and drove to Caherciveen to alert the gardai. Garda Patrick Collins, who accompanied the men back to the strand, found another clear plastic bag inside the brown bag. Local undertaker Thomas Cournane removed the baby's body to his funeral home in Caherciveen and Sergeant Paddy Reidy prayed for it.

Dr John Harbison, the state pathologist, travelled to Killarney next morning to perform a post mortem examination on the Caherciveen baby. He found that it was full term and had lived for possibly twenty-four hours. It had been washed after birth and was up to four days dead. It had a broken neck and had been stabbed twenty-eight times on the chest and neck, and he concluded that it had died as a result of four stab wounds to the heart. He reported that the baby had been "most definitely killed by someone obviously in a state of frenzy or panic, and possibly deranged".

Samples were taken for forensic examination and a full-scale murder investigation was set up. Members of the Dublin-based Garda Technical Branch (also known as the Murder Squad) led by Detective Sergeant Joe Shelly, travelled to Caherciveen. Intensive local activity, including house to house inquiries, produced no results during the following week but the Murder Squad had cast its net wide and soon the investigation switched to the county capital, Tralee, where a twenty-four-year-old unmarried mother who worked as a receptionist at the town's sports centre had come under suspicion.

She was Joanne Hayes, a diminutive girl of four foot eight inches who lived with her eleven-month-old daughter Yvonne on her family's farm at Droumcunnig, Abbeydorney, less than five miles from Tralee. It was known that Joanne had been having an affair with Jeremiah Locke, a twenty-eight-year-old married man, during the previous two years and that Locke was the father of Yvonne. A small, sturdily built man of five foot two inches and eight-and-a-half stone weight, Locke worked as a caretaker at the sports centre. His wife Mary was expecting their second child very soon.

Investigating detectives discovered that Joanne had been visibly pregnant in mid-April but had no newly born child. She had, however, been a patient in the maternity unit at St Catherine's Hospital, Tralee, for a week in April. A scan done at the hospital had revealed that she was no longer pregnant.

The investigation team, now led by Detective Superintendent John Courtney, head of the Investigation Section of the Garda Technical Branch, moved to Tralee and on the evening of 30 April, Joanne's twenty-fifth birthday, it was decided at a conference held at Tralee garda station that she and members of her family should be questioned. Jeremiah Locke would also be interrogated. Next day, 1 May 1984, Joanne, her sister Kathleen (30), her brothers Ned (28) and Mike (27), their aunt Bridie Fuller (69), a retired nurse, and Jeremiah Locke were interrogated separately and at length in Tralee and Abbeydorney garda stations. Joanne's mother Mrs Mary Hayes (65) was interviewed at home.

There are conflicting and hotly disputed versions of what took place that day, starting with the issue of whether or not the interviewees had a choice about where they were questioned. The

Hayes family insist that they were not given a choice about going to the garda stations and the gardai are equally adamant that they were prepared to question the various individuals concerned wherever they wished. There is a similar degree of conflict about whether or not the interviewees were being detained that day.

Under interrogation Joanne at first denied that she had been pregnant and then claimed that she had had a miscarriage at home. However, when she realised that she was being questioned about the Caherciveen baby she made a statement admitting that she had given birth to a baby boy on the night of 12/13 April alone in a field near her home and that she had left the baby in a plastic bag in a pool of water on the farm. She did not know if the baby had been alive at birth. She offered to take the gardai to the spot but this was turned down. The gardai did, however, search the area on the farm that they understood she had indicated but they found nothing. For the next six hours she continued to plead to be allowed to take the gardai to the place where she had hidden her baby but each request, at least a dozen according to one detective, was refused.

The interrogations continued and at 8.30 that night, more than eight hours after she had been brought to the station, Joanne made a statement in which she admitted having a baby in her bedroom on the night of 12/13 April and killing it by beating it with a bath brush and stabbing it with a knife.

Kathleen, Ned and Mike Hayes and Bridie Fuller made statements admitting the alleged birth in the bedroom and all except Bridie Fuller described the alleged killing and subsequent disposal of the baby's body in the sea at Slea Head on the West Kerry coast. Jeremiah Locke made a statement denying any knowledge of the birth and subsequent events and he left the station at 8 o'clock that evening.

A special court was convened in the garda station and Joanne was charged with the murder of an unnamed infant between 11-14 April 1984. She was remanded in custody to appear at Tralee District Court on the following morning. Kathleen, Ned and Mike Hayes and Bridie Fuller were each charged with concealment of birth and were remanded on bail to the same court. Mrs Mary Hayes, who had made two statements, was not charged.

After they had been charged Joanne told Kathleen where she had hidden her baby, but Kathleen misunderstood the directions and failed to find the body during a brief search next morning prior to going to court. That morning Joanne gave more precise instructions about the location.

In court Joanne was remanded in custody for a week to Limerick Prison and the others were granted continuing bail for a week. Shortly after her arrival at the prison Joanne was interviewed by a psychiatrist, Dr John Fennelly, who subsequently described her as having been "a very ill girl" at the time.

That afternoon, 2 May, Kathleen, Ned and Mike found what they took to be the hiding place indicated by Joanne and saw that it contained a plastic bag. They told their solicitor Pat Mann who advised them to alert the gardai immediately. Detectives retrieved the bag from the pool of water and inside discovered the body of a baby boy. The pool was exactly where Joanne claimed she had told the gardai it was during interrogation.

The timing of the discovery was a crucial element in the bizarre events of the following twelve months. Nine months later the Tralee Superintendent Donal J. O'Sullivan admitted to the Tribunal judge Kevin Lynch that if the baby had been found a day earlier when Joanne was being questioned (and asking to be brought to the farm) the Hayes family would have been eliminated from the Caherciveen murder inquiries.

Another bitter irony as far as the Hayes family is concerned is the insistence by the gardai that virtually up to the time that they made their statements each of the people being questioned was free to leave the garda station at any time they wished. According to them Joanne could have decided to go of her own accord, nobody would have stopped her. However, Joanne's name and the names of all the others were entered in the station's Log Book on arrival that day — the procedure used when people are in custody.

Now the gardai had another dead infant on their hands and again Dr Harbison was called in. On 3 May at St Catherine's Hospital, Tralee, he performed a post mortem on the Abbeydorney baby, while sixty-five miles away in Limerick the baby's mother was being transferred to St Joseph Psychiatric Hospital because Dr Fennelly considered her to be a suicide risk.

Dr Harbison found that there was insufficient evidence to say if the newly born and normally developed baby had achieved separate existence, nor could he establish the cause of death. The baby had not been washed after birth.

A week later on 10 May Joanne was granted bail in the High Court in Dublin and returned home.

Tests carried out by Dr Louise McKenna at the National Forensic Science Department in Dublin revealed that the Abbeydorney baby was of blood group O and the Caherciveen baby belonged to group A. Both Joanne Hayes and Jeremiah Locke were also of group O and Dr McKenna had found no traces of group A blood on the night clothes or other items removed from Joanne's bedroom.

The professional opinions of both Dr Harbison and Dr McKenna were that Jeremiah Locke could be the father of the Abbeydorney baby but could not be the father of the Caherciveen baby if Joanne Hayes was the mother. The gardai received this information in late May and were faced with a serious dilemma. If Joanne was the mother of the Caherciveen baby, who was the father? There could be no doubt that she was the mother of the Abbeydorney baby, but all the statements referred to only one birth.

Those incriminating statements were the only evidence the gardai had to link the Hayes family with the Caherciveen case. There was also Joanne's original statement about concealing a baby on the farm to consider. That statement had been proved to be true.

The gardai decided to accept both accounts: Joanne had had twins by different lovers of A and O groups respectively. Now all they had to do was prove it. The official garda file compiled by Detective Garda P.J. Browne was colourful in its "Hell hath no fury like a woman scorned" theme and contained the remarkable observation that, "The possibility exists that the baby found at Caherciveen on April 14, 1984, is the baby of Joanne Hayes. The converse probability that it is not her baby is more likely."

Relying heavily on the possibility rather than the probability, the report which was submitted to the Director of Public Prosecutions recommended that charges be brought against Joanne Hayes and her family. Meanwhile, the original charges which had been laid against them on 1 May still stood.

During the summer frequent remands to Tralee District Court posed a continuing ordeal for the Hayes family while their legal advisers awaited the production of the book of evidence by the state.

Sensationally, on 10 October at Tralee District Court all charges against Joanne and her family were withdrawn. Kerry State Solicitor Donal E. Browne told the court that on the instructions of the Director of Public Prosecutions the charges were to be struck out. He had received the following letter, dated 20 September, from Simon P. O'Leary, a solicitor in the office of the Director of Public Prosecutions.

This amazing case has been carefully studied and a consultation was held today with Chief Superintendent Courtney, Detective Sergeant Browne, the Director and the writer. The accused stand charged in respect of a baby which, on the evidence, was not the baby of Joanne Hayes. Even if she were charged in respect of a baby unknown you could not possibly run a prosecution on this evidence. All charges should be withdrawn at the first opportunity.

On 14 October the story broke in the *Sunday Independent* and there were widespread demands from the media and from politicians to the Minister for Justice Mr Michael Noonan for an investigation into the matter. The main question was how could a family have "confessed" to a crime that they could not have committed.

"We were forced and intimidated, we signed under duress," the family explained to the press and on television.

Mr Noonan responded by instituting an internal garda inquiry to be conducted by Chief Superintendents John Reynolds of Limerick and Hugh Sreenan of the Personnel Branch, Garda Headquarters in Dublin. The minister told the Dail that some gardai could face criminal prosecution as a result of the inquiry.

But the inquiry, which started on 15 October and lasted into November, failed to resolve the matter. On the advice of their lawyers the Hayes family and some gardai declined to submit to a question and answer form of enquiry although they did supply statements to the two chief superintendents.

So, the minister announced that a public tribunal would be held, to be presided over by High Court Judge Kevin Lynch. The purpose of the Tribunal would be to investigate the questioning, charging and subsequent withdrawal of charges against the Hayes family. It would commence at Tralee courthouse on Monday 7 January.

An editorial in the December 1984 edition of the *Garda Review* seemed to acknowledge that the force was on the defensive.

> Even though the forthcoming enquiry into the Kerry Babies case will, we hope, establish that the Force's role in that case was bona fide, the somewhat one-sided publicity which it has already got will, no doubt, remain in the air for a long time. The Tribunal of Inquiry which has been set up to look into that sad saga must, however, be welcomed in the very sincere hope that it can get to the bottom of the case to the satisfaction of

the entire public, including the Garda Siochana, and we believe that it will.

It is extremely important if the rule of law is to prevail that the authorities, including the police, must be seen always to be within the law, even when it may sometimes appear inconvenient for them to do so. In spite of our many successful achievements in 1984 it was a year which saw our moral (sic) take a bashing. It was a year in which thousands of hardworking, conscientious and dedicated gardai had to keep their heads down, metaphorically speaking, while bricks flew on radio, on television, in the newspapers and even in the Dail and Seanad.

...So, for the Garda Siochana probably the best thing about 1984 is that it will soon be over.

It will last about three weeks, the media speculated in the cold days of the new year. "I expected to be in the witness box for about twenty minutes," recalls Joanne Hayes. In fact, she spent five days giving evidence, most of it under cross-examination of such depth and intensity that even veteran court observers were moved to anger. Several times the judge granted a recess to enable her to compose herself as she wept bitterly in response to counsels' uncompromising approach. Never before in Ireland had a woman's personal and sexual behaviour come under such public scrutiny in the law courts. On one occasion she ran screaming hysterically from the courtroom and could be heard vomiting in the corridor outside. A doctor was called to sedate her and to report when she would be fit to resume.

Her cross-examination was widely condemned for its insensitivity and lack of compassion by churchmen, politicians, media commentators and representatives of women's groups. Letters of criticism and protest filled columns of the national newspapers and there were reports that one of the lawyers for the gardai was receiving hate mail and threatening phone calls at his hotel.

Abbeydorney neighbours of the Hayes family were appalled at Joanne's ordeal and on 23 January more than sixty of them staged a demonstration of sympathy outside the Tribunal. Next day hundreds of women from Kerry and surrounding counties defied snow and icy roads to attend another demonstration. They were supported by a contingent who had travelled from Dublin. Letters, telegrams, mass bouquets and messages of support for the family poured into the Tribunal offices each day. Massive deliveries of flowers, sent by well-wishers from all over the country, were made twice daily and there was a national appeal to "Send A Flower to Joanne". Public demonstrations and marches were also held in Dublin and London.

On 28 January Judge Lynch, who had received a garda escort from the Tribunal during the women's protest, ordered a ban on further demonstrations and threatened severe penalties for anybody found in contempt of his ruling.

From the start the evidence to the Tribunal perplexed the eager public. Most of the time there was direct conflict between the gardai and the Hayes family. Bitter allegations and obscure and insulting propositions were heard almost every day. Within the Hayes family there was conflict as Mike Hayes and Bridie Fuller, who gave evidence from a wheelchair in Tralee General Hospital, contradicted the rest of the family and said that the baby was born in Joanne's bedroom. In one of the most poignant episodes of the hearing Mrs Mary Hayes declared that if that was their evidence she would have to say that they were committing perjury. The baby was born outside, she insisted.

Throughout the Tribunal the gardai took the line that they believed the Hayes's statements were true; that Joanne had given birth to twins; that her second baby was the Caherciveen baby; or, as Superintendent Donal O'Sullivan suggested, her second baby had been put into the sea at Slea Head and had not yet been found (this was sarcastically termed the Azores Baby by the Hayes's lawyers); that no pressure or intimidation had been used by gardai to get the statements; that while being questioned each of the interviewees had been free to go at any time; and that Superintendent Courtney's instructions were that the family was to be treated with kindness and courtesy at all times. "They were to get kid glove treatment."

Ban Gharda Ursula O'Regan testified that at one stage during questioning Joanne was actually laughing. A detective claimed that she seemed to be sneering at the gardai. Some described her as relaxed and composed, others said she was hysterical in between periods of composure. Her distress in the witness box was described as playacting. She was called a sociopath, a liar and a manipulator of such consummate ability that she had succeeded in misleading the prison psychiatrist.

The garda account of the original reason for questioning Joanne varied a couple of times during the Tribunal. Early on Martin

Kennedy, senior counsel for the superintendents, insisted that she must have known that she was being questioned about the Caherciveen baby, but subsequently the gardai claimed in evidence that she was merely being asked to clear up the matter of her recent pregnancy. On 16 April Judge Lynch shot down that assertion when he described it as "a load of nonsense". They would have been failing in their duty if they had not regarded her as a suspect for the Caherciveen baby at that time, he said.

Judge Lynch impressed observers with his grasp of detail and his memory but he was criticised for giving what was seen as too much latitude to counsel in their examination of Joanne Hayes and Jeremiah Locke. He did, however, make it known that he would not take kindly to any line of cross-examination which "fell on its face" and he quickly discouraged an apparent attempt to cast unwarranted suspicion on neighbours of the Hayes family.

The Tribunal created legal history when the gardai took the unprecedented step of challenging state witnesses Drs Harbison and McKenna, who over the years had given evidence on their behalf in countless murder and rape cases. The gardai also challenged the opinions of a gynaecologist, an oceanographer and a psychiatrist.

The final submissions by counsel for the parties involved commenced on 10 June and ended on 14 June, leaving the judge with the task of unravelling the web of controversy, conjecture and mystery that had been spun before him since that cold morning of 7 January at Tralee courthouse.

The "Kerry Babies" Tribunal or, more accurately, the Kerry Garda Tribunal had been in session for eighty-two days and had heard the evidence of one hundred and nine witnesses. The estimated cost to the state was in excess of one million pounds.

Its cost in psychological terms to those directly and indirectly involved could never be assessed in mere money.

Midway through the Tribunal I had a short conversation with my fellow-townsman Anthony Kennedy, SC, as we were leaving Dublin Castle one day. He asked me if I was covering the hearings for a newspaper. "No," I said, "I'm with the Hayes family. I'm a believer."

"Are you? Good!" He smiled and went on his way.

Being a believer was easy for anybody who knew the Hayes's.

They could be called naive and gullible, suggestible and easily manipulated, as they showed in their dealings with the media, but nobody would believe them to be capable of that kind of violence. There is no dominant force in the Hayes household, no cunning mind or firm hand to plot their daily course. Even since Bridie Fuller's damaging evidence they continued to visit her several times a week in hospital, right up until her death.

Late in the Tribunal I suggested to Joanne that we might write this book. I did so at the suggestion of a mutual friend who felt that in the interests of justice and fair play her story and her family's needed to be told. In the circumstances communication has not been easy and there may be issues that we have overlooked. But we have not intentionally evaded any aspect of the case. We have, however, endeavoured to avoid causing further embarrassment to innocent victims of the affair by not exceeding the limits of intimacy set by the Tribunal itself.

John Barrett,
Abbeydorney, Co. Kerry.

Nell McCafferty, John Barrett and Willie Leahy. (Derek Speirs/Report)

Who's on Trial?

"WHO'S ON TRIAL? Who's on trial?" The chanting women came across loud and clearly angry. They could take no more and I had nothing left to give. I had emptied my soul, and my stomach, for the Tribunal. I'd been verbally bullied in the cause of justice, and now the women of Ireland were demanding an unwritten element of law — FAIR PLAY.

All I wanted was a cup of tea. The Mount Brandon Hotel was only a minute away and I walked, dazed and confused, through these unknown supporters, occasionally shaking a hand and accepting the flowers which were rained on top of me. I was led towards the hotel by my loyal friends who feared that I might be trampled by my enthusiastic backers. Tralee seemed ready to erupt.

The cheers were for me, the kind of reception given to a winning football team, but I hadn't won anything. All I had done was survive. Five days in the witness box were behind me and all my sins had been made public. Yet not all the shame was mine. The public felt that two lawyers had also crashed the barriers of common decency and as I walked my heart warmed to the women's thunderous demand — SHOW YOUR FACE, KENNEDY, SHOW YOUR FACE.

Martin Kennedy, SC, and Anthony Kennedy, SC, had broken my heart and crushed my spirit and the people of Ireland were making their feelings known. Society wasn't prepared to watch the judical process plumb such depths and the outrage had already been expressed in the newspapers and by various public figures.

I received massive support from the public, who were appalled by what they read. Undoubtedly the Kennedys had won the battle. I had collapsed and become hysterical, but deep down I knew I had won the war, for I had told the truth.

I was taking on The System, but I was not alone.

Women demonstrate. (Michael MacSweeney).

Joanne is greeted by women demonstrators. (Derek Speirs/Report).

The Good Life

I AM A PRODUCT of that system, the last of four children of my parents Paddy and Mary Hayes of Droumcunnig Lower, Abbeydorney, County Kerry. I was born on 30 April 1959 at St Catherine's Hospital, Tralee, and I have lived all of my life at Droumcunnig, as indeed did both my parents.

My mother, whose maiden name was Fuller, was born on the farm where we still live and my father's family farm was just a field away. My uncle Tom Hayes farms there now.

I have one sister Kathleen (30) and two brothers, Ned (28) and Mike (27). Our farm of less than sixty acres is fairly typical for the area, although there are several big farms in the parish. Locals say we are among the oldest families in Abbeydorney and many still remember my grandfather Edmond Fuller who was a national teacher at the village school.

When my parents got married my father moved in to the Fuller farm and shared the work with my uncle Maurice. They seem to have had a perfect arrangement with my father doing the tillage work and Uncle Maurice looking after the dairy side of the business.

Uncle Maurice, a heavily built, stocky man, was a peace commissioner and a very popular figure in the locality. He was a bachelor and was intensely interested in the Gaelic Athletic Association and the ploughing competitions that were so much a part of Abbeydorney life. He was also a founder member of the local coursing club and was a secretary of the local branch of the Fianna Fail party for many years.

His influence in the hurling club is legendary and he is credited with being responsible for much of the success that the teams enjoyed during his association with them. He devoted considerable time to encouraging the young lads in the parish to play for the club.

Jerome O'Donovan, our local victualler, claims that one evening Uncle Maurice packed fourteen boys into his Poplar car to take them to a match in Ardfert. "He'd have taken the full team only that we were short one player," Jerome recalls.

During the summer he seemed to be always going to games in the evenings and at weekends. I remember that he took me to my

Mary and Paddy Hayes with Joanne (in her mother's arms), Kathleen, Mike and Ned. (Hayes family)

Maurice Fuller. (Hayes fmaily)

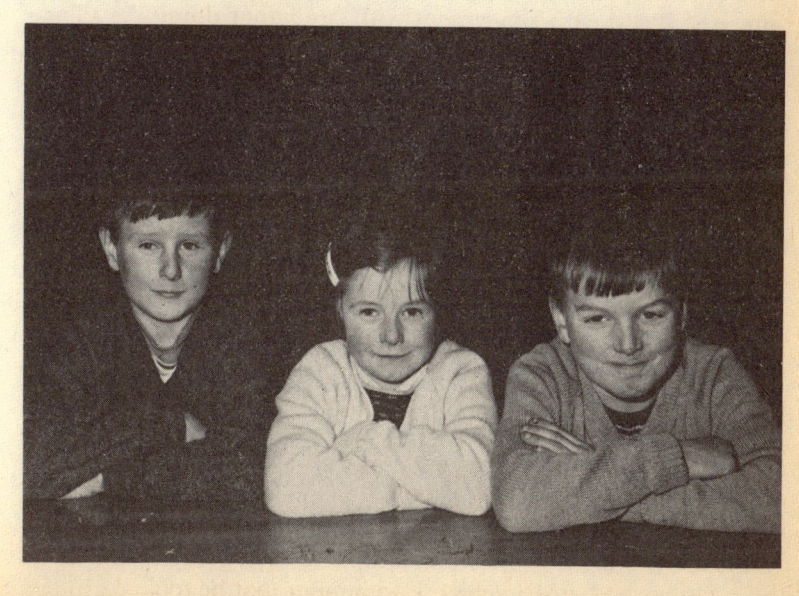

Ned, Joanne and Mike. (Hayes family)

first match when I was very young. During the match one of the Abbeydorney players was sent off the field by the referee and when we came home I told the others the news.

Uncle Maurice was disgusted. "In all the matches I took Kathleen to she never brought home a story like that," he said, as if I was being disloyal to the club by telling the tale in our own kitchen. He really loved Abbeydorney.

His death in 1979 was keenly felt, not alone by our family but by the entire parish. His funeral was one of the biggest ever seen in Abbeydorney.

My aunt Bridie Fuller, who was a nurse, lived with us too. She had qualified in London in 1942 and served as a ward sister with the British Army Medical Corps in Malaya from 1945 to 1947. She came home just prior to her father's death in 1947 and never returned to Malaya. She was engaged to a Scotsman at the time but broke off the engagement and began nursing at St Catherine's Hospital in Tralee. She was assistant matron when she retired in 1978. From my youngest days I remember how we looked forward to her return from work each day because she never forgot to bring us some little treat. We rarely visited the town at that time.

Aunt Bridie was a very popular nurse and after her retirement her steadily declining health became a source of great concern to us and to her many friends. She died in September 1985, not long after the Tribunal ended.

My mother has two remaining sisters, Sr Mary Aquinas, a nun in the Mercy Order, and Joan Fuller. Auntie Aquinas as we call her has been a teacher for over fifty years and is at present attached to the order's convent in the famous holiday resort of Ballybunion. Being so adjacent to home she calls to our house every week and is close to all the family.

Aunt Joan worked in England when I was young and used to come on holiday to Droumcunnig each year. In recent years she has been working as a priest's housekeeper in Newbridge, County Kildare, and she visits us regularly. I have spent many enjoyable holidays with her in Newbridge and in Killeigh and Sallins where she worked previously.

My mother and father were both small and easy-going people who did all they could to provide a happy home for us and to give us the best chance in life that they could afford. Our farm is a mixture of good and rough land and they must have had a real struggle to ensure that we were not deprived of an adequate education and the basic domestic comforts. It was a typical Irish farming home in the sense that for much of the year the work went on each day until darkness intervened and yet the financial return was just about sufficient to pay the expenses. Nobody ever got rich on a small Irish farm.

Religion was an important but unobtrusive factor in our everyday lives. Almost from the time that we could talk we would be helped by Mom and Aunt Bridie to say a prayer before going to bed and of course as we got older our night prayers were extended. Each evening after tea we would all kneel to say the Rosary and Mom would announce the mysteries and lead the prayers afterwards. We still say the Rosary each evening. Like most Irish families we would never dream of missing mass on Sundays and holy days and on the night before there would be arrangements about who would go to first mass and who would wait for second. This was to ensure that there would be somebody available early to milk the cows and feed any dry stock that would need attention, especially in the winter, and those who went to the later mass would do the shopping and get the Sunday papers. On Sundays and holy days only the most essential work, like milking and feeding, would be done as it was considered very important to respect the Sabbath. Most Sundays we would go to a hurling or football match or to the beach if the weather was suitable.

To non-Catholics it may appear that in fact religion did intrude in our lives but we regarded such religious duties as an element in life that was as basic as eating and drinking. Likewise, going to confession and holy communion each month was never seen as a nuisance and we have tried to maintain that practice all our lives. It is an approach to religion which is shared by our neighbours, and I remember well after my First Communion calling around to the houses of friends and neighbours and receiving presents of money from them. I travelled further than that brief trip around the parish when I went up to Dublin to see the Pope in the Phoenix Park, stopping en route at Sallins where my Auntie Joan was working and going on with her then to Dublin.

In my childhood the combine harvester had not yet been introduced so the annual visit of the thresher was one of the highlights of the farming year. Locals would contribute their help willingly on the day of the thresher and also in saving the hay and the men in our house would return the favour for our neighbours. These days involved quite an amount of catering from the kitchen

25

Bridie Fuller and Mary Hayes with Mike, Ned, Joanne and Kathleen.
(Hayes family)

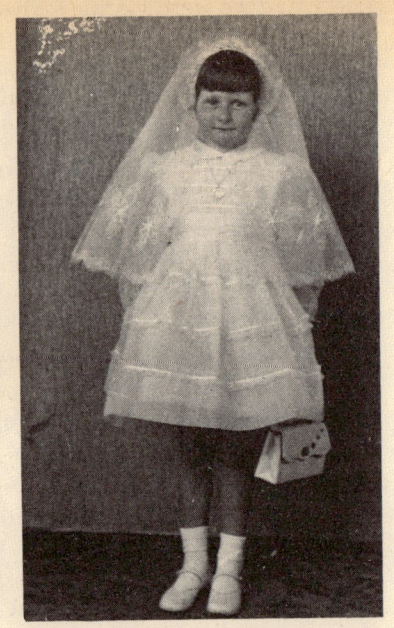

Joanne's First Communion.
(Hayes family)

Yvonne, Ned, Joanne, Mary, Kathleen, Mike. (Michael MacSweeney)

and when we were young we used to love bringing the food to the men in the fields. Days in the bog were also made enjoyable by the picnic atmosphere that was involved and again all the neighbours helped one another in getting the year's supply of turf cut and saved.

Mike, being next to me in age, was my special pal in those days. We made our First Communion together and were always up to devilment like climbing trees or snatching a few apples from an orchard on the way home from school. I know I was regarded as a bit of a tomboy and Kathleen and Ned must have seen us as dreadful nuisances because they were supposed to be minding us most of the time.

Apart from going to the village for a couple of pints at night Dad spent all his time working at home with Uncle Maurice. I remember that Dad slapped me twice when I was very young for being bold and I got a terrible shock because he was normally such a quiet man. I saw him killing a pig once and I hated it. I couldn't imagine how he could do such a cruel thing. But it was all part of country life and I remember that pigs were killed quite often and we would make black puddings and we would eat hardly anything but salty bacon for months afterwards.

As we grew up and learned to play cards there was many a hectic game of 110 in the kitchen before we went to bed. Mom loves a game of cards and she taught us all in our turns but since the arrival of television the cards are rarely produced and "Dallas" and "Dynasty" have taken their place. Nowadays the television is switched on whether we are watching or not; it has become a way of life.

My father's death in 1975 was a terrible shock to me because we had always been very close. I resented his being taken from us and when I think back now I have no doubt that if he and Uncle Maurice had lived just a few years longer I would never have found myself in the trouble which has blighted all our lives.

I suppose the first big event of my life was my introduction to school in 1964. I was among the first pupils at the newly built school in Abbeydorney. Each morning Uncle Maurice would take the four of us and three of the Moore family who lived down the road to school on the horse-drawn cart as he brought the day's milk to the creamery. I can't say that I was ever very fond of school but I didn't have much to complain about either. My first experience of tragedy came in 1968 when my Auntie Annie Shanahan was killed just half a mile from us, knocked down by a car while bringing cows in to be milked.

Abbeydorney is a small but thriving village, just over five miles from Tralee and adjacent to popular tourist resorts like Banna, Ballybunion, Barrow and Ballyheigue. In summer from our house beside the main Tralee-Abbeydorney road we would see a constant stream of traffic as the holidaymakers headed for Ballybunion in cars, on bicycles and with horse-drawn caravans. Because of its proximity to Tralee many locals are employed in the town. The village has two pubs and a community hall and a much admired sports complex which is attached to the GAA pitch. It is a close-knit community in which everybody knows everybody else and is typical of rural Ireland.

I left Abbeydorney school after completing fourth class and started at the Mercy Convent in Moyderwell, Tralee, where I stayed until I had passed my Leaving Certificate just after my eighteenth birthday. My best friend in school was Mary Fitzgerald from Ardfert, whose father was the former goalkeeper for the Kerry football team; she married and moved away to Wexford but we still correspond occasionally and I was delighted to meet her again in Tralee in August 1985. I then did a commercial course at Tralee Regional College and soon got my first job as a supermarket cashier and general shop assistant at O'Halloran's in Oakpark in Tralee. In my teenage years I used to join in the chat about boys and who we liked. Coming from a farm, I didn't have a lot to learn about the basic facts of life: at some time or another you see it all enacted among the animals. Girls weren't obsessed with sex in the way that boys appear to have been. I never heard a girl say that she had had sex or that she would be prepared to do so with any fellow in particular, whereas I have since discovered that boys would boast proudly of such a "distinction" and even lie about it to impress their friends.

My first dance was at a carnival in Abbeydorney and occasionally I would go to a dance in Tralee but generally I stayed at home or visited one of my friends in the village. On my first date with my first real boyfriend, in 1980, we went to an under-14 football match in nearby Finuge; he and I went out for about six months but then we just drifted apart. I played a few games for the Abbeydorney ladies football team when it started first but I wasn't much good at it and after a while my working hours ruled that out. However, I remain very interested in Gaelic football and love to follow the Kerry team, especially in Munster finals and in the All-Ireland semi-finals and finals at Croke Park. Kerry have won two of the three finals that I have attended so, while I regard myself as an unlucky person, I don't seem to have brought them any misfortune anyway. I will never forget the first final I saw, in 1978, because that day Eoin "Bomber" Liston scored three goals and Kerry scored five altogether against their bitter rivals, Dublin. My friend Susie Moore and I had two stand tickets for that match thanks to Uncle Maurice who won them in a raffle. I got a great thrill too at the 1981 final when Jack O'Shea scored a goal at the Railway End right in front of where I was standing on Hill Sixteen. My favourite footballer is Mikey Sheehy who lives on the outskirts of Tralee on the road from Abbeydorney. Another great Kerry player — Ger Power — lives on the same road just two miles from our house. I like hurling too and my favourite team are Kilkenny who, incidentally, wear the same colours and stripes as Abbeydorney.

On 13 November 1978 I made the move that was to have a major impact on my life when I started as a receptionist at the Tralee Sports Centre. This magnificent complex had been open for a couple of years at that time and was a very popular amenity in the town. My wages were £20 per week and Martina Ronan, who later became a close friend of mine, began work in the office on the same day.

The entire staff consisted of: Manager — Michael Moss; Receptionists — Mrs Irene McGaley, Martina Ronan and me; Lifeguards — Mary Murphy (now Mrs O'Riordan) and Aileen Shanahan (now Mrs Enright); Groundsman — Jeremiah Locke. Liam Bohan, who is a former Irish swimming champion, replaced Michael Moss as manager in September 1982.

Jeremiah Locke. (Michael MacSweeney).

Jeremiah

MARTINA AND I were on shift work and our duties involved booking the courts and the swimming pool, occasional typing and making up cash lodgements for the bank. We were kept busy and I enjoyed the work because the patrons were easy to deal with. I rarely availed of the facilities at the centre and still spent most of my spare time at home. In fact I only ventured into the swimming pool once and I often regret having thrown away the opportunity of learning to swim.

From the time that I started work at the sports centre Jeremiah Locke was very friendly towards me and he made me feel welcome straight away. At that time I had a steady boyfriend but after seven months we drifted apart.

I can't remember when I first became aware of any special feelings for Jeremiah. I began to look forward to meeting him at work and always enjoyed his company when he joined some of the other girls and myself for a drink in the evenings.

Transport to and from work was a regular problem for me as I don't drive and I was constantly depending on lifts or on arranging for one of the family to oblige. This wasn't always convenient, especially in the bright evenings when farm work continues until dusk.

I suppose it was inevitable that one day Jeremiah would offer to drive me home and when he did on 26 October 1981, I gladly accepted. We made love that evening, or had sex, as the Tribunal termed it, in the back seat of the car by the roadside near my home. As the world knows I wasn't a virgin then but I wasn't in the habit of having spontaneous sex either. These things don't just happen, Martin Kennedy, SC, asserted at the Tribunal, and he was right. I was ready for Jeremiah's approach and after that evening I was uncontrollably in love. However, I must say, in extenuation of my behaviour, that I was in no doubt that Jeremiah was unhappy in his marriage. If I had thought otherwise there would have been no sex and no love, no Yvonne and no Tribunal.

This still does not justify my willingness to have an affair with a married man, but at least it clarifies the situation as I saw it at the time.

For the next twenty-six months I became the classical "other woman", without the rewards of a mistress or the rights of a wife. Our rare public outings together were confined to a drink with friends in Tralee or a visit to a pub in a remote North Kerry village, and even then we would be uneasy and fearful of being recognised. At Christmas 1981 he gave me a gold cross and chain and the next Christmas he gave me a gold bracelet. In early 1982 Jeremiah's wife and her mother came to my workplace to speak to me, but I wasn't there. Then in the autumn his wife and I had a fearful row in the toilet at the sports centre.

My behaviour defied all the strictures of my upbringing and family background. I had no right to love him as I did or demand his love in return and I ignored the advice of my family and friends, whose wisdom I should have respected. I accept the blame but I hope there will be some who will understand, and even admit that, but for a bit of luck or a quirk of fate, they too could have taken a similar path to self-destruction.

I was happy to snatch an hour with Jeremiah whenever the opportunity arose. It was never the sordid sexual affair that was painted at the Tribunal. Our times together were blissfully happy and I was deeply in love. I welcomed my first pregnancy in 1982 and was very upset when I had an early miscarriage at work during the June Bank Holiday.

Two months later I was pregnant again and Yvonne was born on 19 May 1983 at St Catherine's Hospital in Tralee. I was delighted to be pregnant again but my family were very upset at first, especially when I told them that I was determined to keep the baby. They wanted to have the baby adopted but I wouldn't listen. I told them they could throw me out if they wanted to but they never threatened such extreme action and they accepted her happily when she was born.

Jeremiah offered to contribute towards our baby's upbringing but I told him I would look after her myself. He visited me once while I was in hospital after the birth.

I called her Yvonne because I liked the name. In Irish she is called Siobhan, like myself. My brother Ned and my sister Kathleen are her godparents and whatever misgivings my family may have had prior to the birth there is no question of their love and devotion to her now. It is a great source of happiness to me that they are so attached to her.

Jeremiah, on the other hand, has never shown much interest

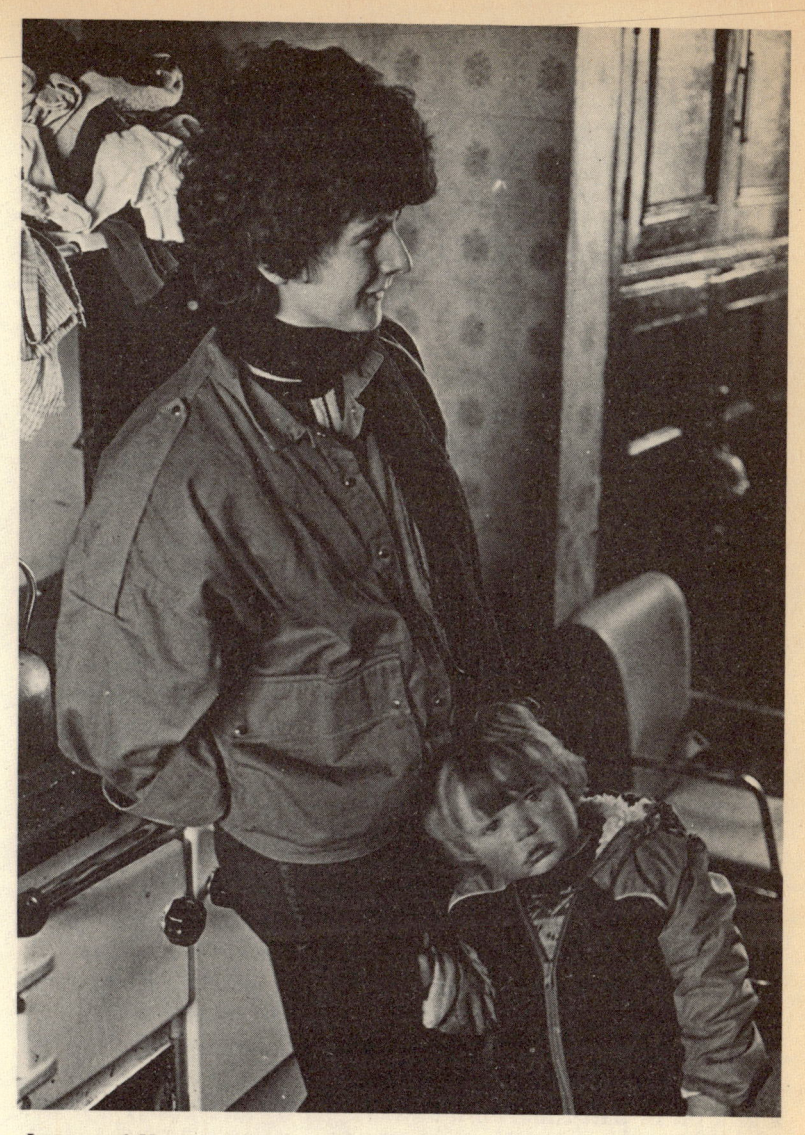

Joanne and Yvonne at home. (Michael MacSweeney)

in her and this has always disappointed me. In fact it was his failure to inquire about her after she had been to Cork for an operation on her finger in February 1984 that finally ended our relationship. We spoke subsequently at work but we were always cool towards each other.

As far as I know he has only seen her twice in her life and has never sent her a birthday card or present.

I got leave from work a month prior to Yvonne's birth and returned to duty in July. The novelty of having a baby in the house was a joy we all shared and the family's initial embarrassment was soon dispelled. We brought her to the village when we went shopping and were delighted when our friends fussed over her.

Jeremiah and I resumed our relationship despite the strong opposition of both our families. His wife had given birth to a baby before Yvonne was born and some of his family had caught us in his car and abused us and had called to my house to complain angrily to my mother. Liam Moloney, the Abbeydorney garda, spoke to me about it at the request of my family but I rejected his advice although, in my heart, I knew that Jeremiah would not leave his family now.

So when I discovered in October that I was pregnant again I was disappointed, although, of course, I could hardly say that I was surprised. I have been asked many times why we weren't using contraception in view of our precarious situation. The truth is that we never considered it. I was deeply in love and to use contraception merely to have sex would have been placing a barrier where emotionally I felt none. My commitment was total and unlimited. Contraceptive facilities were available but we didn't consider using them and it is ludicrous to suggest that the Catholic church's opposition to contraception had anything to do with it. By falling in love with a married man I had broken one of the church's cardinal rules anyway.

This pregnancy was a serious worry because I felt I could not expect my family to accept a second child by this married man of whom they did not approve. My friends too would be disappointed, especially those who didn't like Jeremiah anyway. I decided to keep my situation a secret while I pondered my future.

I knew that I would have to give up my job and that I would probably have to get a flat in Tralee. With social security allowances and a bit of part-time work I would get by all right. Yet it was going to be a big break for me and I became terribly depressed. As far as I was concerned the world had caved in on me and everything and everybody was against me. I became paranoid and felt that everybody was watching me and that my condition was noticeable long before it was, so I began wearing loose clothes to hide my condition.

Jeremiah was the first to hear about it, but not in the joyful way that I had told him about my previous pregnancies. We were at a pre-Christmas staff party at a hotel in Tralee and one of the girls whispered to me that his wife was pregnant. I was shocked and bewildered by the news. This was the ultimate rebuttal of what I had been led to believe during the previous two years. I told him that I wanted to see him for a minute in the car park and I asked him if it was true. Yes, it was true.

I told him that I was pregnant too and we had a bitter row. Eventually he said he was going back to the party, and as he walked away my creaking world fell apart. The cherished dreams had been mere illusions after all.

I know that I was being selfish and unreasonable in my attitude, but the sense of betrayal I felt at the time is difficult to convey. I was deeply in love and I had thought that he felt the same about me. I simply couldn't accept that I wasn't the only woman in his life. I had been living in a fool's paradise but I was on my own now, another casualty of loving not wisely, but too well.

We went out for a drink a few times during the next two months but we were never intimate again after that unforgettable December night.

Christmas is always a sad time for me ever since my Dad died but Christmas 1983 was terrible. Yvonne was too young to enjoy it, although we all bought her little toys and new clothes, and my mind was preoccupied with the terrible secret I was carrying. I prayed for guidance to take the right decision, for the courage to tell somebody.

They used to talk about procrastination at school, the definitive word for putting things on the long finger. I became a procrastinator, postponing from day to day the disclosure of my condition. I had many friends to confide in, loyal people who have supported me through several crises since. I should have told my family. They would have been disappointed in me, but they would not have let me down.

Yet I continued to run away from my problem. If I ignored it, I thought, it would go away. If I didn't deal with it it would never happen.

Several times I came close to breaking the news but I always hesitated. I'd tell somebody tomorrow, it was always tomorrow; but tomorrow never came. My boss Liam Bohan and my friends Mary O'Riordan and Martina Ronan mentioned it to me when

I was at an advanced stage of pregnancy but I wasn't yet prepared to discuss the matter. I gave them the impression that the birth would be in June and that everything was under control. I didn't want to reveal my helplessness or trade on their sympathy and I didn't want to hear any criticisms of Jeremiah either. If somebody had said "I told you so" I would have screamed.

How many times since have I cried and blamed myself for not revealing the truth! So much would have been different, a life might have been saved and I and so many others would have been spared the turmoil that the Tribunal was to bring. But it's easy to be wise now!

In fact, apart from knowing that the baby was due in April, I had not calculated a precise date and it was that lack of foresight that was to prove so disastrous in the end. I had decided on less important details like calling it Shane if it was a boy or Noreen if it was a girl but I remained vague about the actual date of birth. I know in my heart, despite the assertions made at the Tribunal, that if my labour hadn't started so suddenly and unexpectedly I would have sought help in the final days. God, why should I seek revenge for my problems on my own defenceless baby?

I had known the joy of having Yvonne and having experienced the delights of motherhood I could never wilfully harm another baby. To me, this is the all-important issue of the entire affair. I need to be believed that I meant no harm to that baby. I can accept criticism of my morals and insults to my personality but I swear again, as I have sworn many times already in public, that I never intended to harm that baby and that, as far as I know, I wasn't responsible for its death. I couldn't live with that kind of guilt.

Thursday, 12 April 1984, was my day off work and I did some washing for Yvonne, as I do most days. I felt relaxed and comfortable all day despite the worries which were piling up. In the evening I watched television and a neighbour Molly Kearney called down to see Mom, who had the 'flu. Kathleen went down the road to the hairdresser Helen Lyons to get her hair cut.

Yvonne was troublesome about going to bed but after Kathleen came home she persuaded her to go.

It was around bedtime, I'm not sure of the precise time, that I began to feel hot and flushed but I didn't take much notice because there was a 'flu in the area and the kitchen was warm. I got ready for bed, but then I began to feel hotter and I went out the front door to get some air.

Alone in a Field

I WALKED AROUND wearing only my nightdress and dressing gown. I was still feeling feverish but there was no pain. It had to be the 'flu. I was so hot, but there couldn't be labour without pain. I was still walking around when I felt a numbing sensation, as if I got a punch in the stomach, and then without warning the waters burst. Now in the open field I realised that the birth was imminent. My secret was still a secret and I was utterly alone.

I don't know how quickly things happened after that but the baby came very soon, so unexpectedly in fact that it was born as I was standing up and I felt hardly any pain at all. I pulled the baby's head as it emerged and prayed to Our Lady as I was giving birth. Suddenly the baby was on the grass with the umbilical cord attached to it and to me, internally. I pulled the cord and it broke. The afterbirth came almost immediately, I'd say. I didn't even think of it. I didn't think of anything. I don't believe I blacked out, yet even now I can't remember thinking constructively or rationally.

Worst of all, even to this day, I don't know whether the baby was alive or not. Thankfully the pathologist could find no evidence that it had achieved life and I console myself with his expert opinion.

I remember hearing Kathleen calling from the house to ask if I was all right, and I replied that I'd be in in a minute. I must have sounded reasonably coherent because she believed me and went to bed. I left the baby on the ground and went in and took off the nightdress and dressing gown. They were covered in blood. I got a clean nightdress from a trunk, went to the bathroom and washed myself and put on the nightdress. I put away the bloodstained clothes and went to bed.

Kathleen was sleeping on a mattress on the floor of my bedroom, because Mom was sleeping in the house. Normally Mom sleeps in the cottage about a hundred yards from the farmhouse but because of her 'flu we had brought her down so that we could look after her. Yvonne was asleep in her cot in my room.

In bed I was tired and worried, physically drained rather than sleepy. There was no question of sleeping, although I could hear

Kathleen snoring nearby. The enormity of what had happened began to dawn on me. The baby was my biggest worry. Had I harmed it? I tried several times to go out but I hadn't the courage. I was afraid of what I'd find, so I just kept turning it over in my mind as if it was all just a terrible nightmare that would eventually go away.

I got up at around 5 a.m. and went to the kitchen. Auntie Bridie was up and we had tea, and then I went out again in only my nightdress. I may have taken a flashlamp but I'm not sure. I picked up the baby without really looking at it and I took it to the corner of the field and covered it with hay.

I went to bed again and tried to decide what I would do with the baby. I wasn't sore, or even as tired as I should have been in normal circumstances, but I was frantic for a solution to my problem. Evasion was an obsession with me.

I would say it was about 7.30 a.m. when I got up again. This time I got a brown paper bag and a plastic bag from the press under the television and went down the field to where I'd left the baby. It was bright now and it was then that I saw it was a boy. I put the baby into the paper bag and then into the plastic bag and climbed over an old iron frame of a bedstead that was being used to block a gap in the ditch. I walked around, searching for somewhere to hide it, and I saw this pool of water and I put it in there and then I returned to the house, never once looking back to where I had placed my little bundle.

I went to bed again and probably slept for a while, but I remember telling Ned to ring the sports centre to say that I wouldn't be going to work. I was due on duty at 3 p.m. I also told him to phone Auntie Aquinas and Auntie Joan to tell them that I was sick because normally on Thursdays or Fridays, depending on whether I was working, they'd ring me or I'd ring them. We used to take turns at phoning each other.

I spent most of the day in bed and had tea a couple of times but I didn't eat anything. When I got up that evening I felt weak and was losing a lot of blood. Kathleen had found the afterbirth in the field during the day but hadn't mentioned it to me as she wasn't sure what it was. Now, however, she noticed that I wasn't looking well and she walked a mile to my cousin Ted Shanahan's house to ask his wife Mary to come down to see me.

Fortunately, Mary's friend Elsie Moore, who is a nurse, was visiting the Shanahans at the time and she accompanied Kathleen and Mary to our house. They were alarmed at my appearance and I told them I had had a miscarriage. They insisted that I should see a doctor straight away but I didn't want to go, although I was feeling very low now.

They phoned Dr Daly in Tralee and he said I should come in immediately. Reluctantly I agreed to go with them and after I'd met the doctor he ordered me to hospital.

I refused to go to hospital that night because I didn't want to leave Yvonne. I suppose deep down I thought I might be dying and I was afraid to leave her. I spent another sleepless night at home and next morning Ned drove me to St Catherine's Hospital in Tralee.

I was put to bed in the ante-natal clinic and I told the doctors and nurses who examined me that I had had a miscarriage, or thought I had. I received blood a couple of times and everybody was very kind to me. Even after I had had a scan I tried to mislead the doctors into believing that I had had a miscarriage and I am really ashamed for having done so.

It was while I was in hospital that I read in the local weekly newspaper *The Kerryman* of Thursday 19 April about the finding of a baby at Caherciveen. My recollection is that I got a shock when I read it, although there was no reason why I should because I knew it wasn't my baby. Was it some kind of premonition about later developments or am I only imagining that sense of shock now, in view of what has happened since? I simply don't know.

I improved fairly quickly in hospital and I was discharged on Easter Saturday, 21 April. It was Yvonne's first Easter and we got her Easter eggs and tried to make a fuss of her, although of course she didn't understand what was going on.

Physically I felt all right again but I was very depressed and worried. Deep down I wanted my baby to be found because I knew I'd have to live with my terrible secret until it was. I could never again go down to that part of the farm while the baby was there.

I remained home on sick leave for another week, taking Yvonne for walks and calling to neighbours. I tried to behave as normally as anybody would who had just been discharged from hospital after having a miscarriage. I was still putting on an act.

I returned to work on Monday, 30 April — my birthday — and resumed my usual duties. I told the girls that I had lost the baby and gave the impression that it had happened while I was in hospital. Some of them blamed me for not letting them know I had been in hospital, as they would have visited me, and I told them I hadn't wanted any visitors as I had been very depressed.

Next day, 1 May, I had been at work for just two hours when the police walked in. It was exactly 12 noon and I was typing in the office when I saw a man approach the reception window. I thought he might be looking for the manager but to my surprise he asked me if I was Joanne Hayes.

I recognised him as Detective Tim O'Callaghan before he introduced himself and I then saw that he was accompanied by another man who said he was Detective Con O'Sullivan.

They asked me if they could have a word with me and I went outside with them. When we were outside they asked me to accompany them to the garda station to answer some questions. I went back to the office and told Irene McGaley that I'd be back in a few minutes. I thought they had found my baby in the field at home in Abbeydorney. Outside I saw Jeremiah Locke getting into a car and I was going to get in beside him but I was told I would have to go in another car, which was parked nearby.

I was driven to Tralee garda station and when I got out of the car I felt everybody in the street was looking at me, although nobody could possible have known what was going on at that stage. It is a strange irony that I had always wanted to see the inside of a garda station — Abbeydorney's is hardly more than an office.

I was led upstairs to what I later discovered was the superintendent's office. It was a big room — I thought it was a conference room — and very soon Garda Liam Moloney, our local garda in Abbeydorney, came in. I was sitting down, one leg tucked up under me as I always sit, and as I looked out the window I saw my brothers Ned and Mike walking into the station.

I asked Garda Moloney why the lads were there and he told me all my family were being brought in for questioning. I knew Garda Moloney fairly well as he had been a frequent caller to the house when my Uncle Maurice was alive. Uncle Maurice, being a peace commissioner, used to have to sign forms and various documents for the gardai. There was also the time he had called on me about my relationship with Jeremiah.

Now he was questioning me about my recent pregnancy and for about an hour I denied that I had been pregnant or had given birth to a baby. I'm fairly sure he mentioned the Cahercivcen baby early on but at any rate when he again mentioned it, I told him the truth, that I had given birth to a baby alone in a field on the farm and that I had hidden it there.

Being accused of having any connection with the Caherciveen baby was a shock that I hadn't been prepared for and I became really frightened when I saw that he didn't believe my true account of what had happened.

Ban Gharda Ursula O'Regan came in and I repeated my story to her but she didn't believe me either, although Garda Moloney did make a note of it.

Garda Moloney asked me if I'd like a cup of tea, and Ban Gharda O'Regan went out and brought back some tea and buns.

I was drinking the tea when I encountered Detective Superintendent John Courtney of the Murder Squad for the first time. It was an unforgettable experience.

Detective Superintendent John Courtney. (Michael MacSweeney).

Interrogation

MY FIRST REACTION to Detective Superintendent Courtney was to recoil from him. He is a tall broad-shouldered man with the weather-beaten countenance of a farmer or fisherman. I had never heard of him but from the moment that he faced me in that interview room all I knew was instant fear, a terrified, instinctive reaction to those piercing, deep-set, half-closed eyes and the thin lips that seemed to spread right across his face.

I didn't know who he was when Superintendent Courtney walked into that room in Tralee garda station but I sensed danger. He wanted the truth, no covering up for anybody. He knew the facts so for my own sake I'd better tell the truth. He said threateningly that he'd be back.

Within five minutes or so he was gone, presumably to apply his gruff aggression elsewhere. I never met him again but he made a lasting impression that remained right through to the end of the Tribunal more than a year later.

He was leading the investigation into the murder of the Caherciveen baby and, being a native of Annascaul, was operating almost on his own West Kerry doorstep. He was head of the Investigation Section of the Dublin-based Garda Technical Branch or Murder Squad and he had brought several of his troops with him to assist in the investigation. As Superintendent Donal O'Sullivan admitted in evidence to the Tribunal, they are known in the force as the "Heavy Gang".

When the Murder Squad go into action they like to describe it as assisting the local gardai in their investigations although as was shown at the Tribunal they take over the operation. The local gardai more or less confine themselves to carrying out the squad's instructions and providing facilities like transport and equipment.

The official garda account for our presence in the garda station on 1 May was that at a conference held on the previous evening it had been decided that we should be "invited" to the station or to anywhere else we might prefer to go to explain my recent pregnancy. So Jeremiah and I were picked up at the sports centre and Kathleen, Ned, Mike and Auntie Bridie received their "invitations" at home at the farm.

The superintendent's instructions had been emphatic, stressed the Tribunal gardai. We were to be treated with kindness and courtesy. They called it "kid glove treatment".

By early afternoon we were all, except Kathleen, being interrogated simultaneously in separate rooms at the station in connection with the murder of the Caherciveen baby. Kathleen was taken to Abbeydorney station and questioned there before being driven to Tralee later that evening. Mom was interviewed at home where she was alone with Yvonne.

During the Tribunal the gardai couldn't quite make up their minds about whether or not we were being questioned about the Caherciveen baby.

In January, cross-examining me, Martin Kennedy, SC, was in no doubt. When I told him that I had thought that day that my baby had been found in Abbeydorney, he asked me if I had read about the Caherciveen baby in *The Kerryman* newspaper and did I not think it much more likely that that was what they wanted to talk to me about.

"Was it not obvious they wanted to talk to you about the Caherciveen baby?" he demanded. I replied that it had never dawned on me.

Later in the Tribunal the gardai denied strongly that we had been brought in in connection with the Caherciveen baby and they insisted that they had merely wished to clear up the question of my recent pregnancy. The judge listened until apparently he could take no more. "I think that is a load of nonsense," he declared.

There was serious conflict too about the question of whether or not we were in custody that day. The gardai were in no doubt — we were free to go at any time we pleased up to the time that we made our incriminating statements.

If we were free to go why wasn't I taken out to the farm to show where I had hidden my baby? They didn't deny that I asked several times. One of the answers given to that question by one of the Heavy Gang was that the superintendent didn't want me to be upset. In a different setting that reply would have been good for a laugh.

Jeremiah Locke, who was at the station until after 8 p.m., told the Tribunal that he would have gone home at 2 o'clock if he had been allowed. He had asked if he could go, but he had been refused, he said.

The gardai, on the other hand, said Jeremiah refused to go home because he was worried about what he would tell his wife. This assertion seemed to suggest that once outside the station he had nowhere else to go except home and discounted the possibility that he might have had several other places that he could visit.

If we were free to go why did Garda Moloney deem it necessary to telephone a neighbour to ask him to milk our cows that evening?

Why was another garda sent in to stay with us whenever an interrogating garda wished to leave the room?

"In case anything would happen to them," Ban Gharda O'Regan explained.

What could happen to Bridie Fuller, for instance?

"People have been known to jump through the windows in garda stations," the Ban Gharda replied without a trace of a smile.

"Do you seriously suggest that Bridie Fuller, at the age of seventy, would have jumped out the window?"

A significant aspect of our presence in Tralee station on 1 May was the fact that all our names were entered in the Log Book as we came in or were inserted later as omitted entries, which is the precise procedure used when people are in custody. While we were being questioned other gardai were taking statements from our friends and working colleagues.

The gardai never came up with a satisfactory explanation for those facts.

Certainly some of the counsel were not impressed.

Kevin O'Higgins, SC, for the Attorney General, asked one garda witness if he was seriously suggesting that any of the people being questioned could have got up any time and said, "Right lads, that's all for today, I'm off to the pictures", and they would have been allowed to go.

"That's right," replied the witness.

Dermot McCarthy, SC, wanted an explanation for the way the station appealed to people. "Apparently when ye bring anybody in there ye can't get them to leave the place," he told a witness, in undisguised sarcasm.

At any rate, I can only say that I wouldn't have delayed too long about getting out of that station if I had been given the opportunity.

I had given Garda Moloney and Ban Gharda O'Regan a true statement about the birth of my baby at the farm and now I was confronted with members of the Technical Bureau, the Heavy Gang, whose chief was Detective Superintendent Courtney.

It was a long and gruelling session and I knew that I didn't stand a chance unless I could convince them that my baby was at home on the farm at Abbeydorney. Then at least they would realise that I had nothing to do with the Caherciveen baby.

Time and time again I pleaded with them to take me home so that I could show them that I was telling the truth but they wouldn't listen. They weren't writing down what I was saying either. One of them said he would organise a search and I prayed that they would find the baby but after a while he told me that the search had been fruitless. They weren't surprised but I was devastated.

The pressure was unbearable. They wanted the "truth", the version that would fill the gaps in the scenario they had created. I had nothing to fear, killing a baby wasn't considered to be murder any more. It was called infanticide now, they said.

But I knew nothing about the Caherciveen baby and I couldn't help them. I cried out that I couldn't help; they decided that I wouldn't, and the pressure became more intense. I held out until I could take no more, then I delivered the statement that they had been after all along and suddenly they couldn't write fast enough. In my abject misery I had at least made them happy. They had chalked up another victory for the Heavy Gang.

They took me down to see Auntie Bridie and I told her what I had said in my statement. I encouraged her to do the same, so that she could be allowed home. I was responsible for the others being in the situation in the first place, so now I would take the blame.

By the end of the night, all of us had signed statements and each of us, apart from Jeremiah, had been charged. I was charged with murder, and Kathleen, Ned, Mike and Auntie Bridie were each charged with concealment of birth.

The incriminating statements which led to the charges being preferred against us have been a major source of conflict between my family and the gardai. We have insisted that we were forced and intimidated into making those statements and the gardai have strenuously denied our allegations. As it was those statements and our charges in relation to them that provided the major issues to be decided by the Tribunal, I have reproduced them in full in an appendix at the back of the book.

The statements contradicted each other in a number of ways. In what they had to say about who was in my bedroom when the baby was supposedly born there: my statement had only Aunt Bridie with me, as did Bridie's statement; Kathleen's had her, Aunt Bridie, Mom and Mike; Mike's statement said he was not there, while my mother's had her, Aunt Bridie and Kathleen there.

There were discrepancies in the times at which the car was supposed to have returned from Slea Head and as to who went in the car and as to whether the baby was placed in the boot or on the floor of the car.

There were discrepancies about the kind of bags into which the baby was said to have been placed, with various combinations of white plastic, grey fertiliser, blue manure, clear plastic, brown shopping and turf bags. Also there were differences as to who supposedly placed the baby in the bags.

In the statement I signed it was I who supposedly got the bathbrush and knife, in Kathleen's she got the knife, and in Mike's, Kathleen got the knife and the bathbrush.

There were discrepancies as between statements and it also became clear later on that assertions in them conflicted with clear forensic and other evidence. In my statement, for example, it said that I stabbed the baby in the back; yet the Caherciveen baby had no wounds in the back.

As our solicitor Patrick Mann wrote to Mr Brian Curtin, BL on 15 August 1984, "The entire Hayes family say that the statements which the Guards took off them were taken by intimidation and they have nothing whatsoever to do with the birth of Joanne's child, and the statements that have been taken off them have to do with the Caherciveen child which was found on the beach there. Therefore, it would seem that there are good grounds for contesting the statements."

Slea Head. (Michael MacSweeney).

Detective Garda P.J. Browne and Detective Sergeant Gerry O'Carroll. (Michael MacSweeney).

In Prison, Hospital and the Courts

AT A SPECIAL court in Tralee garda station at 11.05 p.m. on 1 May 1984, I was charged by Detective Sergeant Kevin Dillon with the murder of an unnamed male infant between 11-14 April and remanded in custody to appear at Tralee District Court on the following morning. Then I was escorted to the Day Room by Ban Gharda O'Regan.

Mike was sitting there and Superintendent Donal O'Sullivan told us we could talk if we wanted to but I was crying and I don't think we said anything. Mike was too frightened to talk to me anyway.

Ned was the last to give his statement and this was completed just after 1 a.m. Eventually I met all the family in the Day Room. Like me they were shocked and distressed, shattered by the incredible developments of the previous twelve hours. They had their charge sheets in their hands and presented a pathetic sight as they awaited the next move. They too had been remanded to the District Court of 2 May.

Kathleen whispered to me that the statement she had given was "all lies", and I said "the same here". We were frantic to know if Mom and Yvonne were all right at home.

I think it was Superintendent O'Sullivan who told me that the others were being allowed home and when I realised that they were going without me I got very upset. I tried to tell Kathleen where I had hidden my baby before they were ushered out to a police car. Until then she had thought I had lost the baby in hospital. They still had to break the news to Mom that I had been held in custody and had been charged with murder.

Mom says that Yvonne clung to her all that night as if she sensed that something terrible had happened. Each time Mom tried to take her to her cot she screamed and Mom had to abandon the idea of getting her to bed. She was still in Mom's arms when the others arrived home at about 1.15 a.m.

I was taken to a cell by Ban Gharda Teahan (Maher) and I

remember thinking that if only I could somehow get to Banna Strand I would drown myself. I was to think of Banna many times in the days that followed.

I don't remember much about the cell except that there was a stone slab covered by a bit of foam to sleep on and there was just one blanket. Ban Gharda Teahan offered me more blankets and I was glad to accept two more because I was shivering from the cold and desperately tired.

I must have slept for a while, although I remember hearing a male prisoner in another cell getting sick several times during the night.

At some stage Garda Declan Liddane, whom I knew as a patron of the sports centre, brought me a cup of tea and I appreciated this very much because he was pleasant to me and a friendly face in the frigid atmosphere that prevailed was worth a lot.

For breakfast a garda brought me a mug of tea and some bread and butter in a kind of shoe box. I refused the bread but drank the tea and when the garda went out I heard somebody say "Better throw your man a bit of bread," which I presumed referred to my fellow prisoner.

Shortly afterwards I had a surprise and welcome visit from Garda Bill Cregan, whom I also knew through my work. He shook my hand warmly and wished me luck. It was a brave and typically kind gesture from a man who had the rare ability to allow his humanity to supercede his garda status.

Some time that morning I was asked if I wished to contact a solicitor to represent me in court and for the first time I was inspired to do something for my own good. I asked the gardai to contact Patrick Mann, a local solicitor who had been in private practice for just a few years, to act on my behalf. I had known Patrick casually as a patron of the sports centre and I thank God now that I remembered to ask for him as not alone has he represented me and my family ably and diligently at all times, but he has proved to be a true friend in the most demanding situations.

He never lost patience or talked down to us and was always available when we needed him. Right to the end of the Tribunal he maintained his confidence in us and never failed to offer an optimistic side to the blackest situations. His parents and family also supported us generously from the start and made us welcome in their Abbeyfeale home many times.

I met Patrick for a few minutes before the court started and he told me I would probably be remanded in custody but that he would arrange bail for me as soon as possible.

Kathleen told me that she had failed to find the baby and it transpired that she had misunderstood my directions. She promised to search again when she got home and I prayed that it had not been moved or disturbed by animals. It was a gruesome prospect that I hadn't considered previously.

To my relief the others were again granted bail but, as Patrick had indicated, I was remanded in custody to Limerick Jail for a week, to appear again at Tralee District Court on the following Wednesday. He asked me to name two people who would be prepared to go bail for me and I cried and told him that nobody would be willing to give money for me.

Subsequently our good friends Jerome O'Donovan, a victualler and the man who succeeded my Uncle Maurice as peace commissioner of Abbeydorney, and Paudie Fuller, a farmer from Kilflynn who is a cousin of ours and was then a member of Kerry County Council, offered to act as bailsmen.

I was taken back to the garda station and given a meal but I could only pick at a beefburger. Food was the least of my worries as I spent my last hour in Tralee for only God knew how long. Eventually a taxi arrived and I was placed in the back seat with Ban Gharda O'Regan. A garda sat in front with the driver.

I was heartbroken now, as if my links with home were finally severed while every mile took me farther away from those I loved. The two men were talking about cutting turf, and I remember Ban Gharda O'Regan telling me not to be crying; "It's no use now!" Such a remark was as futile as slapping a child to make it stop crying. This was one order I couldn't obey.

During the journey, and especially going through the city of Limerick in my last minutes in the free world, I remember envying the people I saw chatting or strolling around on their casual business.

Limerick Prison is a terrifying place even from the street. I saw the huge grey walls and the rolls of thorny wire that linked those awful boundaries to the outer railings. Ban Gharda O'Regan handed me over to a female warder and I was led to a pre-fab building inside the railings.

I was searched and my bag and watch and money were taken from me. The dehumanisation process was under way. Soon I would be a mere statistic with, presumably, a number rather than a name. I was warned not to reveal what I'd been charged with because my fellow prisoners would not take kindly to a child murderer. There would be no point in telling them that I was innocent or that I'd never been to Caherciveen, or Slea Head either. For my own protection I was to lose, or at least not reveal, my identity. The prison was to protect society from me but it couldn't guarantee my safety inside those walls — not as the notorious Joanne Hayes anyway.

A warder produced the biggest bunch of keys I had ever seen and opened the main gate. Inside I saw another massive gate, just as the first one thudded shut behind me. I will never forget the rattle of those keys or the sickening impact as the gates closed on the outside world. In an office they counted my money and put away my belongings. I thought of Yvonne: oh God, may she never know such heartbreak and humiliation.

We walked across the big yard, the high walls of this living tomb provoking the first signals of the claustrophobia that I dread. I was glad to reach the women's section, relieved to be away from that awful yard. In my real world such open spaces were green or sprouting vegetation. I was guided down a long corridor, our footsteps echoing in the eerie silence. The lady governor, a small, dark-haired woman, spoke to me but I couldn't hear. Maybe it was she who told me not to talk about myself to my fellow prisoners. I don't know.

Then I was weighed and measured, vital statistics to go into some kind of national record. Two warders led me away to have a bath. They set up a screen around the bath and waited outside and when I was finished they told me to wash the clothes I was wearing. I was given a bra and panties and jumper and skirt but they allowed me to keep my shoes. They were slip-ons and regarded as harmless because they had no laces.

I dressed in the ill-fitting clothes. At only four foot eight inches, I am not easy to fit. I didn't worry about hygiene or what kind of girls had worn these clothes before me. The spirit soon succumbs to the reality of the situation. Servility and futility are the dominant elements, you don't need a mind of your own. You are not required to make any constructive contribution so you can concentrate on yourself and your fears and your sense of desolation.

Was it fear that made me feel so weak as we climbed the stairs to the cells? Later I discovered that the stairs were indeed frighteningly high and I used to dread using them. We stopped at a door and I saw the peephole in the centre. I hadn't noticed any other prisoners yet, although they may have been peering out at the new arrival as I passed. Or did they not care any more?

They opened the door to my cell, a long narrow little room that seemed to be filled by the chair and table and bed. Up high, almost at the ceiling, there was a window. There were bars on the window.

I was alone now and terrified, although the door was not locked. Soon I would be like Lassie our sheepdog. Get up, Lassie. Lie down, Lassie. Come here, Lassie. Lassie spends much of her time in our kitchen and she does what she's told. But if she wants to go out she only has to walk towards the back door and one of us will open it for her. A dog's life had its advantages if you looked at it from a prison cell. God, not alone was I confined but I didn't even know the time. What harm could I have come to with a mere watch?

I lay on the bed, crying and lonely, and after a while a warder told me the governor wished to see me. I was taken to her office and I was introduced to a doctor whom I later knew to be Dr John Fennelly, a psychiatrist at the nearby St Joseph's Psychiatric Hospital and visiting psychiatrist to the prison. He talked to me in the presence of the governor but I haven't the slightest recollection of anything he said. It was a brief conversation anyway and before long I was back in my cell once more.

Dr Fennelly told the Tribunal that at the meeting he had found me distressed, with suicidal tendencies and that I was in a highly suggestible condition. I was "a very ill girl", he said.

At some stage, a warder brought me a few books. No doubt she meant well but I was in no mood to appreciate love stories. Mills and Boon belonged to another era, a time of my life that now seemed beyond recall. I must say that I found the prison officers kind and understanding and not at all like they are generally portrayed on the screen. The ban ghardai that I encountered could have learned a lot from them.

Eventually I met a prisoner for the first time. She came to my cell and introduced herself and said it was time to go down for something to eat. By a remarkable coincidence I met that girl again ten months later after the Tribunal had been moved to Dublin. Kathleen and I were having a meal at the Ormond Hotel where we were staying and the girl came to our table and wished us luck. To be honest I didn't recognise her. She told us that she had been on remand when I was there and that she had recognised me subsequently from pictures in the papers. I never asked her for her name, nor did I enquire about her problem, but I do hope that she has managed to stay clear of trouble since then.

The food was on a table on a landing and I saw the girls helping themselves to chips and beans and tea and bread. There were ten or fifteen prisoners, all of them young, and they were chatting in groups as they selected what they wanted to eat. I remember the shock of discovering that only plastic cups and plastic cutlery were available. It wasn't that I had never drunk from a plastic cup before but now the lack of choice was a grim reminder of the fundamental reality of my situation.

I didn't talk to anybody. I put a few chips and a small portion of beans on a plate and poured a cup of tea for myself and took them back to my cell. I didn't eat the food — it looked cold and burnt and I wasn't hungry anyway, but the tea was welcome.

Later a warder asked me to go out for some fresh air but I couldn't face that yard again so I refused to go. I stayed in the cell, pining for home now, praying that they were all alright and that Yvonne wouldn't miss me too much. I got another cup of tea before we were locked up for the night and I was given a nightdress. I was dreading lights-out time and was immensely relieved when a warder asked me if I'd like to keep the light on in my cell. She must have noticed that by now I was terrified.

I slept a few hours that night because I was totally exhausted. I don't know if they looked through the peephole at me but I suppose they did. I had a cup of tea next morning but again I stayed clear of the other girls.

I wasn't long back in the cell that Thursday morning when I was ordered once more to go to the governor's office. There I met Dr Fennelly again and he told me that he was transferring me to a hospital. St Joseph's is just down the road from the prison and on the way I asked the driver of the prison van if this was an ordinary hospital and he said it was. I think I signed myself into the hospital, although I may be totally wrong as I was still very much a prisoner. I signed something at any rate.

I was taken to a general ward which contained about fifteen patients and again I was warned not to mention the murder charge. The nurse who accompanied me told me to tell the other patients that I was in for treatment for depression.

The staff were exceptionally kind to me and for the first time in several days I managed to eat a meal. Yet I was still very depressed and worried. Not knowing how they were faring at home, whether Yvonne was all right, and not being able to contact them was a constant torment. I was interviewed regularly by Dr Fennelly and by several other doctors and their kindness and sympathy always made me feel better, if only for a while.

I became friendly with three of the patients and they too helped to raise my spirits. One of them, an alcoholic, was a natural comedienne and did a lot to take our minds off our own problems. I was helped also by the relaxed atmosphere. The freedom to make tea or help ourselves to a snack at any time was greatly appreciated.

It was while we were having tea in the lounge on the Thursday evening, 3 May, that I learned for the first time that my baby had been found on the farm at Abbeydorney. In fact we had turned down the sound on the television, and it was on the tape used for "News for the Deaf" that I saw it. None of the other patients passed any remarks. I was relieved and yet I felt more helpless than ever for I had no way of communicating with anybody who might have been able to tell me of the significance of the discovery. Still, it was consoling to know that at last I had been vindicated and that there could be no question of my involvement in the case of the Caherciveen baby now.

I was still charged with murder and incarcerated in a hospital where every patient appeared to have a psychiatric problem. It was a grim situation but I could answer for my own baby and prepare myself to take the consequences. I never dreamed that the gardai were about to come up with the "Twins Theory"!

Early on the Saturday afternoon my aunt, Sr Mary Aquinas, and another nun came to see me and within minutes my mother, Kathleen, Ned, Mike and Auntie Bridie arrived, having been driven from Abbeydorney by local shopkeeper Francie O'Donovan.

I was very nervous at first because I didn't know what they would say to me. They were entitled to blame me for landing them in trouble and for having ignored their advice but, thank God, they were loving and kind from the start. Once we got talking it was like a family reunion and I gave them tea and toast and they stayed for about an hour.

It was then that I heard that the baby had been buried the previous day in my father's grave in Abbeydorney and that the burial had so nearly taken place at Rath in Tralee, presumably in an unmarked grave. Garda Moloney and a detective had called to our house at 2.10 p.m. to say that the baby was in Gleasure's Funeral Parlour in Tralee and that the burial would take place at

Rath at 2.30. He asked if Mike, who was in the house at the time, would attend. Ned had taken our car to the village a few minutes earlier.

Luckily Francie O'Donovan arrived to deliver a message just as the two gardai were leaving, and when he heard about the arrangements and saw that Mom was upset, he volunteered to contact Gleasures and to have the grave dug in Abbeydorney. So the burial took place in our own grave after a Tralee priest had prayed over the baby in the mortuary. Kathleen, Ned, Mike, Francie O'Donovan, Hannah Moore (one of our neighbours) and two detectives were present. The local priests weren't available — Fr Hickey, our parish priest, was ill at the time.

The family were happy that the ceremony had been carried out privately but, unfortunately, a photographer later took photographs of the grave and these were published in the following day's papers. This hurt my Mom deeply and still upsets her whenever it is recalled. It was the first intrusion of this kind by the media, but in subsequent months we were to endure a constant onslaught by people who were only interested in getting their story or photograph, regardless of our feelings or wish for privacy. Sometimes we were forced to stay inside the house while photographers took up position on the road outside, ready to pounce if one of us should appear. Poor Yvonne spent many a sunny day indoors because of them.

Such problems were far from our minds that day as we chatted in the hospital. Francie O'Donovan promised to bring them to visit me again on the following Monday but I was still very lonely when they were leaving. I would have given anything to be able to go with them, to see Yvonne even for a few minutes, but I was glad to hear anyway that she was getting on well without me.

An hour later Patrick Mann arrived, jaunty and confident as ever. I didn't know that Patrick had been told by a doctor on arrival that I was still deeply depressed and he was to do his best to avoid discussing the case with me. I couldn't understand why he kept changing the subject whenever I tried to talk about it. He told me he was arranging bail for me and was trying to locate a peace commissioner in Limerick. He didn't stay long but he did tell me that Jeremiah wasn't very popular in Tralee.

He brought me letters and a box of chocolates from some of my friends and when he left I read in one of the letters that Jeremiah was going through a bit of an ordeal. I decided to write to Liam Bohan, my boss, because I was afraid that Jeremiah might lose his job. Ironically I had been due to sit for an examination on 19 May with a view to being made permanent in my position. Martina had been made permanent as a result of a similar examination in February. I knew that my days at the sports centre were over now, but apart from being worried about Jeremiah's job I felt that I owed Liam Bohan an explanation anyway.

I wrote:

Dear Liam,

I don't know how to start this letter. I am so sorry for causing such an embarrassment to all of you working with me. Please forgive me. I want to thank you for the help you have given me since you came to the complex. You were new there when I first got pregnant, but still you never said anything to me.

Don't ask me why I did what I did, because I don't know, or I will never know. I am so ashamed for what I did, and most of all I am so sorry for getting everyone I love involved. It must be all the pressure building up that made me do it. I really don't know. When the Gardai took me down to the station on Tuesday they were delighted because, according to them, they had the murderer for the baby in Caherciveen.

I had to make a false statement because they told me if I didn't my mother would be jailed and Yvonne would be put into an orphanage. I am now in a hospital for mental cases. Am I mental, Liam? I can't think straight any more. I don't mind being punished for what I did, but I don't want to be punished for the baby in Caherciveen.

Mr Mann came to see me today. He told me Jer is having a pretty rough time around the town. Please, Liam, don't be too hard on him. I have ruined his life also. I really love him.

You are a real nice person and thanks for everything you did for me. Say a prayer for me.

Love,
        Joanne.

I also enclosed a letter to Jeremiah, saying that I loved him and apologising for the fact that he was getting a rough time on my account.

Liam came to Limerick to see me later in the week. He subsequently told the Tribunal that he had regarded my letter as "a cry for help". I suppose it was, in a way.

As promised, Francie O'Donovan brought Kathleen, Mike and Auntie Bridie to visit me again on the following Monday. This was a very emotional meeting because with every passing day I could see less hope of a solution to my problems.

Francie and Kathleen located a peace commissioner to witness my signing of an affidavit which Patrick Mann had sent to me concerning my application for bail. Again they tried to keep me from talking about the charges and the terrible situation we were in and I found this very frustrating, but they were acting on instructions from the doctors and instead they talked on any random subject they could think of.

By now I had developed something of a routine at the hospital, starting the day with mass at the chapel in the hospital grounds and taking regular walks, always escorted by a nurse. Each day too a nun, Sr M. Consilio from the local Presentation Convent, would call to see me and I looked forward to her visits. We talked about my situation and my past behaviour but she was never critical, nor did she try to lecture me, and I grew very fond of her.

On Wednesday I was driven to Tralee District Court for my remand appearance. Before we left Limerick I was taken to the jail first to be searched which was a severe jolt to me because by now I had more or less deluded myself into thinking that I was a hospital patient rather than a remand prisoner.

I was driven in a big black car to Tralee accompanied by a driver, a garda, a ban gharda and a nurse, Sheila Vaughan, a lovely person who couldn't have been more kind. Facing into my own town in such circumstances should have been a daunting experience but somehow by the time we reached the courthouse I didn't care.

There was a number of curious spectators in Ashe Street when we arrived but I took no notice of them. Remarkably I felt much more upset by the onlookeers during the Tribunal, although by then I was no longer charged with anything.

Having been remanded in custody for another week, I was allowed to meet my family in a small room at the courthouse and Patrick Mann assured me that my application for bail at the High Court in Dublin on the following Friday would not be opposed. I also met Martina Ronan, Peggy Houlihan, Judith Hayes and Breda Murphy, my former sports centre and VEC staff colleagues, and it was really heartbreaking when I had to leave them and face the journey back to Limerick once more.

I hadn't seen Yvonne because my family felt it might upset her and it would certainly have been distressing for me, although I longed for even a glimpse of her every minute I was there.

We drove straight to Limerick Jail where I was searched again and the prison officer inquired if we had stopped for something to eat on the journey. We hadn't of course and it was too late then to do anything about it, but when we got back to the hospital Nurse Vaughan cooked chips and sausages for me and I settled in to look forward to the bail proceedings that would ensure my release on Friday.

I was dressed and ready for the journey to Dublin at 4.30 a.m. on Friday and a nurse was informed by the jail that I would be collected at 6.30. I was to appear at the High Court at 10 a.m. I started to grow very uneasy when nobody had arrived by seven o'clock and an hour later I knew something had gone wrong and I became hysterical at the thought of having to remain in custody.

At 10 a.m. I was allowed to phone Patrick Mann at his Tralee office and he was shocked to hear that I was still in Limerick. However, with typical assurance he told me there was "no problem". He would see that things were taken care of in Dublin and I ended up the conversation hopeful, if not entirely convinced, that I could still be free by evening.

In Dublin it was arranged that my bailsmen Jerome O'Donovan and Paudie Fuller would bring the bond to Limerick Jail, and I received a telephone call that they were on their way. I still shudder when I recall those agonising hours as I waited for them to arrive. Every kind of possible mishap passed through my mind.

I will never forget the relief when I was told to gather my belongings and prepare to go to meet them. At 5.30 p.m. I was taken to the jail and we signed the bonds that were my passport to freedom, however temporary. The bail terms were: two sureties of £5,000 and my own personal surety of £100 and I was to report to Tralee garda station every Monday between 9 a.m. and 9 p.m.

I was given a voucher for the bus journey home and I remember that I was terrified that the bus conductor might ask embarrassing questions in front of the other passengers, but he understood the situation and never said a word. On the way home Jerome and Paudie warned me a million times that I was to have no contact with Jeremiah. If I did my bail would be revoked and I would get no second chance.

At home we had an emotional reunion, hesitant at first, and then everybody seemed to be talking at the same time. Yvonne was asleep in her cot but I picked her up and hugged her until she woke and recognised me. It was a night of wonderful relief but I could sense the fear that had enveloped the family and the house itself. We were still facing serious charges although we now felt certain that it would only be a matter of time before they would be withdrawn.

Frequently during that lovely summer we appeared at Tralee District Court to be granted further remand. Our case was usually called first and we would leave as soon as the remand had been approved. Occasionally Patrick would ask about the availability of the book of evidence and the usual reply was that it would be ready within a month.

Every Tuesday, Kathleen and I would hand in our dole forms at the Abbeydorney garda station but neither of us ever said a word to Garda Moloney.

At home we tried to carry on as best we could in the circumstances. It was desperately embarrassing when my friends called to see me. At first I didn't want to meet them and I couldn't bring myself to look them in the eye, but gradually that passed and we got back on our usual terms again.

In July I went on an all-night vigil to Knock Shrine in Mayo and placed my entire destiny in the care of Our Lady. If Our Blessed Mother couldn't help me I was doomed I felt, and I have always believed since that it was her intervention that saved me from being convicted in the wrong.

Mom asked our local curate Fr Nolan to say mass in our house, but he declined and offered to say mass at Kilflynn chuch, which is not our local church. We were disappointed but not really surprised. However, in February, we did have the privilege of having mass celebrated in our house by a visiting priest and each of us took an active part in the service. Unfortunately we could not invite our neighbours because the priest did not wish our local clergy to hear about it in case they might be offended. We will always be grateful to the priest who fulfilled Mom's dearest wish.

To our joy Yvonne walked for the first time in August. She took those first faltering steps in our own kitchen and we were all delighted that she had at last passed that barrier even if she was a bit late at sixteen months. Unfortunately Auntie Bridie's health deteriorated during the summer and she spent several months being transferred between hospitals in Cork and Killarney and Tralee.

My main concern during those months was that the Caherciveen baby mystery would be solved. It wasn't that I wished the mother of the baby any harm or sought revenge for what I had been through because of her and any accomplices she may have had. I simply wanted to have the terrible worry of the charge lifted from me and the family.

Unknown to us it had been an uncomfortably hot summer for our adversaries in the Murder Squad. The Director of Public Prosecutions and the Kerry State Solicitor Donal Browne were not impressed by Detective Garda P.J. Browne's 130 page report, colourful and imaginative though it undoubtedly was.

On Wednesday 10 October we attended Tralee District Court in anticipation of another remand. We were sitting in the courtroom when Patrick Mann came in and said that he had got a "whisper" that there might be a happy development in store. He said no more and we were on tenderhooks as the court started and the acting garda officer asked for a further remand for all of us. Patrick told the judge that he had heard that the state might not be proceeding with the case and he asked if Mr Donal Browne could be requested to come from the nearby Circuit Court.

The judge said he would let the matter rest until Mr Browne could attend. Now the tension was becoming unbearable. Eventually, Mr Browne arrived and informed the judge that he had been instructed by the Office of the Director of Public Prosecutions to withdraw all charges against me and my family immediately. It was a marvellous moment for us even though the full significance of the announcement took a while to sink in.

We nudged one another and filed out of the courtroom to savour the freedom we had been granted in the less austere surroundings outside. There were groups of troubled people huddled in various parts of the foyer waiting their turn to be called before the bench but we were gloriously unburdened at last and we were at the giggly dividing line between laughing and crying. I remember swearing to myself as we walked down the courthouse steps that as long as I lived I would never again set foot in that building.

Four days later, 14 October, reporters Don Buckley and Joe Joyce broke the story in the *Sunday Independent*. Actually, there had been television and radio advertisements about the article during the two preceding days so we were prepared for the newspaper coverage. The story was immediately taken up by political and civil rights interests and the Minister for Justice announced that he was initiating an internal garda inquiry, to be conducted by two chief superintendents.

Next day, 15 October, we had our first encounter with the national media when we were asked to appear on the RTE current affairs programme *Today Tonight* to discuss our experiences of the preceeding six months. We agreed, subject to the consent of Patrick Mann, and this programme was broadcast on the following night. On 25 October we again appeared on *Today Tonight* and at that time we were also interviewed by journalists from the national papers. The twin issues of our "confessions" and our allegations of intimidation against the gardai had aroused tremendous public interest.

Soon we were requested to appear before the garda inquiry but we refused to submit to a question and answer session, as indeed did several of the gardai involved. The Minister for Justice had said that prosecutions could result from the inquiry and we were advised that we were in no way obliged to comply with the superintendents' request. As Kathleen said in evidence, we had seen enough of gardai at that stage.

However, we did supply written statements of our allegations and experiences with the gardai to the chief superintendents. Predictably, the garda inquiry failed to provide the answers that the minister sought and on 11 December he announced that he was setting up a Tribunal of Inquiry. High Court Judge Kevin Lynch would preside and the hearings would start at Tralee courthouse on Monday 7 January.

What is a tribunal? we asked ourselves. There would be no wigs and gowns, Patrick Mann assured us, which made it appear less intimidating than it sounded. According to the terms of reference our role would simply be to help the judge decide about the events at Tralee garda station on 1 May and the subsequent withdrawal of the charges that had been made against us.

I began to socialise again on the insistance of my friends who assured me that I had no reason to feel embarrassed. My problems were behind me and I couldn't stay in hiding forever so I went to a disco most weeks and often went for a drink or to music sessions in Tralee. I was gradually escaping from the depression that had threatened to destroy me and I was greatly encouraged to find that the public didn't regard me as a freak to be observed from a distance, or as an undesirable who should be ostracised. Being treated as an ordinary human being can be a tremendous boost when you've emerged from my kind of situation.

Once the Tribunal was out of the way I would organise my life either in a new job or as a full-time mother to Yvonne. Spring would be in the air and the politicians were already talking about "building on reality". I would do just that. I would make the most of my potential and forget the past. Roll on the Tribunal; things could only get better.

The Tribunal Starts

Tribunal Personnel

Dermot McCarthy, SC, and Brian Curtin, BL, for the Hayes family, instructed by Patrick Mann, Solicitor, Tralee.

Martin Kennedy, SC, and Brendan Grogan, BL, for Superintendent John Courtney, Dublin; Superintendent Daniel Sullivan, Caherciveen; Superintendent Donal O'Sullivan, Tralee; instructed by Thomas O'Dwyer, Solicitor, Dublin.

Anthony Kennedy, SC, and Paul Gallagher, BL, for twenty-five gardai based in Dublin and Tralee, instructed by Donal Courtney, Solicitor, Killarney.

Kevin O'Higgins, SC, and James Paul McDonnell, BL, for the Attorney General and the Director of Public Prosecutions, instructed by the Chief State Solicitor's Office.

Michael Moriarty, SC, and James Duggan, BL, on behalf of the Tribunal, instructed by Michael Buckley, Solicitor, Chief State Solicitor's Office.

Terms of Reference

To enquire into and report to the Minister for Justice on the following matters of urgent public importance:

(1) The facts and circumstances leading to the preferment on May 1st, 1984, of criminal charges against Joanne Hayes, Edmund Hayes, Michael Hayes, Kathleen Hayes and Bridie Fuller, Droumcunnig Lower, Abbeydorney, Co. Kerry, in connection with the death of an unnamed infant and subsequent events which led to the withdrawal of those charges at the Tralee District Court on October 10th, 1984;

(2) Related allegations made by Joanne Hayes, Mary Hayes, Edmund Hayes and Michael Hayes in written statements to their solicitor on October 23rd, 1984, and by Kathleen Hayes in a written statement to her solicitor on October 24th, 1984, concerning the circumstances surrounding the questioning and the taking of statements from those persons on May 1st, 1984;

(3) Any matters connected with, or relevant to the matters aforesaid, which the Tribunal considers it necessary to investigate in connection with their inquiries into the matters mentioned at (1) and (2).

Martin Kennedy. (Michael MacSweeney)    *Judge Lynch.* (Michael MacSweeney)

Brian Curtin, Patrick Mann and Dermot McCarthy. (Derek Speirs/Report)

THE EDGINESS SET in around Christmas. This time the Tribunal was the spoilsport as we contemplated the prospect of having to go public with our allegations about the gardai. We hadn't asked for such an airing of our grievances and we had no choice as regards giving evidence. Any reluctant witnesses would soon have had their minds changed for them by way of subpoena. We had nothing to worry about but we knew that a lot of painful and embarrassing memories would be rekindled and we had already suffered enough pain and embarrassment during the preceding eight months.

Half an hour before the Tribunal started we met our senior counsel Dermot McCarthy and barrister Brian Curtin for the first time. The introductions in Patrick Mann's office, just a hundred yards from the courthouse, were informal and friendly, almost lighthearted in fact. We were blissfully ignorant of the trauma that lay ahead of us and to be honest we revelled in the first-name relationship that was immediately established with the eminent lawyers.

I have been asked how we would have fared with some of the other legal figures involved in the Tribunal who might have been less receptive to our uninhibited approach. If they didn't like it they could lump it as far as I'm concerned. I would never defer to people by calling them Mister or Miss on the basis of class or social distinction.

Both Dermot and Brian proved staunch and able representatives, suffering when we suffered and beaming their delight and encouragement when we had had a "good" day. Dermot might give the impression of being fussy and always in a hurry but we found him patient and prepared to listen to anything we might have to say even when he was up to his eyes in transcripts and legal documents. He worried constantly about us during our stay in Dublin and his repeated warnings not to go near O'Connell Street became something of a joke between us. Often when I spoke of Yvonne he would talk about his own little daughter, "the boss of the house" as he called her.

Brian, whose home is at Lisselton near Ballybunion, is almost a neighbour of ours. Built like a rugby forward, his dry sense of humour endeared him to us from the start. Despite his protestation he enjoyed our teasing about his ongoing battle against the flab and would proudly give us a progress report when his dieting was yielding results. One lovely evening in May he took Kathleen and me to the Spring Show at Ballsbridge and afterwards treated us to a meal at Killiney.

With less considerate legal representatives our Tribunal ordeal could have been immeasurably worse, yet when I reflect on that first meeting between us I can't help wondering if the odds weren't stacked against us from the start. If we had been in a position to pay our own legal costs we would undoubtedly have arranged to meet Dermot and Brian long before the Tribunal began. This would have given them a chance to assess us and to brief us about what we were about to face.

We knew nothing of court or tribunal procedure. Things like direct evidence and cross-examination were legal jargon beyond our comprehension, terms we would skip over in a newspaper report. Because we were on legal aid, or hoped we were, we were a family at the mercy of the bureaucrats who signpost everybody's way when the state is involved. It was literally a case of "Don't call us, we'll call you." We were allocated lawyers to represent us and didn't even have the guarantee that our costs would be paid for us. That would be at the judge's discretion at the end of the Tribunal. If for any reason we hadn't liked the lawyers who were nominated to represent us that, presumably, would have been our hard luck.

It would be extremely naive to suggest that the gardai and superintendents didn't meet their legal representatives until the opening day of the Tribunal.

Walking towards Tralee courthouse that Monday morning we didn't dream that such a nasty and bitter confrontation lay ahead. The hearing was expected to last three weeks and we would simply have to answer a few questions about our allegations against the gardai. The photographers came to meet us as we approached the building. Across the street some locals lounged against the shopfronts, waiting to size up the cast before deciding about going in. The photographers were mostly new to us, although we recognised a few familiar faces among them. The television men would come right up to you, almost as if they were looking for blackheads or pimples on your face, and then they would back away in front of you as you walked. We found them intrusive and unrelenting especially since Mom can walk only very slowly and we had no chance to escape them, but after a few days we accepted that they had a job to do and we established a friendly relationship with them.

Even as we took our seats in the front row of the crowded public gallery the battle lines were drawn. The gardai were grouped on one side, we and our friends sitting across from them. Ahead of us were the immaculately dressed lawyers and their assistants. They had their backs to us so we couldn't get a good look at them. It would take us a few days to get to know their names and to discover whose side they were on. Without their court garb they looked deceptively ordinary, the kind of fellows you could meet any day in the street.

We saw the Kennedys, who were representing the "defendants", gardai and superintendents. Martin, big and bulky and in his fifties, towered over his younger namesake, the dapper Anthony. As they took their places side by side that morning we had no inkling of the hurt and heartbreak we would experience as a result of their questions on behalf of their clients. Later I grew to detest even the sound of their voices and found it extremely difficult to remain in the Tribunal room when either was speaking.

Just in front of the lawyers, to their left, was the chair, the seat of torture for me and my family and friends. A microphone was conveniently set up to amplify our anguish. On both sides of the courtroom dozens of media representatives sat poised to deliver the Tribunal titbits to the world outside. Some left when they had no more to feed to their voyeuristic readers; others who were concerned with the real issues remained to the end.

A long high bench fronted the painted wall ahead of us. "Silence," ordered the court attendant and the chatter stopped instantly. Everybody stood up and instinctively I put my hand to my forehead to bless myself as you do when the priest comes to the altar to commence mass. I stopped my hand in mid-air and got my first glimpse of Judge Kevin Lynch: inscrutable face, dark hair circling a bald dome, and wearing a stylish pin-striped suit. He bowed to the gathering and sat down behind the bench to put the Tribunal in session.

Michael Moriarty, SC, in his polite and somewhat monotonous tone, opened the proceedings with a detailed background to the case and, to my horror, he named Jeremiah Locke as the father of Yvonne and as the man with whom I had had a long relationship. I had hoped that he and his family could have been spared the distress that such a disclosure would bring and soon afterwards I was shocked to learn that he would in fact be called to give evidence.

I heard John Griffin describe the finding of the baby in Caherciveen and listened to the details of the stab wounds with the detatched revulsion felt, no doubt, by every other woman in the court. It was shocking but, frankly, it had nothing to do with me.

They were talking about somebody else's baby. Its mother was hundreds of miles away perhaps, with a terrible secret that had yet to be unearthed. Was she by now shaking at every knock on her door? She must have been on everybody's mind that morning. Even then I didn't know that the gardai still insisted that they had their killer and that she was sitting only yards away from them.

Liam Bohan, my former manager at the sports centre, was the first witness of my acquaintance. He said he had been made aware of my affair with Jeremiah through gossip at the centre and recalled telling me that I was entitled to maternity leave just I had been granted when I was expecting Yvonne. He said that from February 1984 onwards it had been quite obvious that I was pregnant. "It was not a balloon she was carrying under her jumper," he said bluntly. It was distressing to hear Liam reel off instances of my attempts to deceive him and my colleagues and I became very upset when he produced the letter which I had written him from hospital in Limerick. When I heard that letter read out in public all the misery that I had felt when I was writing it flooded back to me. I cried bitterly, but if I felt humiliated by such revelations in public I had some harsh realities to discover as I went along.

Mary O'Riordan, or Murph as we call her, suffered visibly in the witness stand as she spoke of being surprised when I told her the true story of having had my baby in the field. Obviously she was disappointed that I hadn't confided in her but she said she would not hold it against me as I had been through a very hard time. She had taken Yvonne and me to her home in Tralee for a day late in April after I had phoned her when I was very depressed. She was my loyal and close friend and now she was being asked to denounce me as a liar and totally worthless individual.

I can never speak highly enough of her support and kindness to me during the Tribunal. Her husband Tom had been a garda in Listowel and Tralee and they both knew all the local gardai

Martina Ronan, Mary O'Riordan and Joanne. (Derek Speirs/Report)

involved in the case. Tom had since taken up a career in insurance but it can't have been easy for them to back me so openly in the circumstances. Yet they never wavered. Each day while I was in the witness stand Murph sat conspicuous and unreservedly supportive, smiling her encouragement to me to keep going. After each day's hearing she would accompany me to a local hotel or bar for tea and following my most distressing day in the witness box she forced me to spend the night at her home. During the Tribunal she began receiving obscene phone calls, sometimes in the early hours of the morning, and she was deeply upset but nothing would deter her in her support for me.

Martina Ronan, another loyal friend and former colleague, was questioned about my affair with Jeremiah. She said she knew something was going on between us and she was not aware of my going out with anybody else. She did not see any reason why I should have told her lies and, yes, she was surprised that I had done so.

God, I thought, why hadn't I confided in these dear friends!

Slowly and solemnly Martin Kennedy cautioned Martina to think carefully before answering his next question. Did the name Tom Flynn mean anything to her?

"No," Martina replied. It meant nothing to me either.

Only Martin Kennedy appeared to attach any importance to the question at the time, but if that little scene could be replayed now it would cause a national outburst of laughter. The serious aspect of the question was that Mr Kennedy was actually launching the search for my (non-existent) second lover that would vindicate the subsequent introduction of the Twins Theory.

Dr Louise McKenna, the forensic scientist, had found the name Tom Flynn written in biro on the side of a mattress taken from my bedroom and had passed on the information to the gardai. The mattress had been bought, second hand, by my Auntie Bridie in McElligott's shop in Castleisland some years previously and using their assessment of me as a yardstick the gardai had come up with the idea that this would have been a likely location for me to write the name of a boyfriend. Each time the name was mentioned the public laughed and soon youngsters in Tralee were wearing T-shirts inscribed "I Am Tom Flynn".

There would be no limits where I was concerned. The most preposterous theories would be presented to try to prove that I was the ultimate in promiscuity, if not exactly a prostitute. The Tribunal would delight the voyeurs of the nation with the facts of my internal organs, sometimes in centimeters, always in gory detail. Thanks to such revelations and allegations I and at least one of my friends received disgusting letters from kinky individuals from as far away as the United States. And from Cork a man who claimed to be in the entertainment business would offer me "five hundred to a thousand pounds a week" to take part in whatever kind of entertainment he was engaged in. I hope that by not replying to his letter I managed to convey the contempt with which I regarded his approach.

That Tuesday my former working colleagues John Walsh, Irene McGaley, Peggy Houlihan and Aileen Enright joined Martina on the growing list of people who had never heard of Tom Flynn.

Poor Peggy must have wondered if she was in a court of morals after she had admitted in evidence that she had a drink one day in Tralee with Jeremiah Locke. Drinking with a married man, tut-tutted Martin Kennedy, to the absolute disgust of all who know Peggy and her husband Frank. Taking Mr Kennedy's reaction into account it was a relief later on to see some of his colleagues bravely and openly sharing a table with women journalists in the cafeteria at Dublin Castle, but it would be wrong of me to say for certain that by that time he had dropped his guard and actually joined them.

In retrospect Aileen Enright's evidence underlined the inconsistency of the whole concept of tribunal or court evidence. She is a qualified nurse who used to meet me every day at work. Most days we had lunch together. She told the Tribunal that she noticed that I was pregnant in December 1983. The judge asked her if she had formed the opinion that I was pregnant with one baby. Indignantly Anthony Kennedy asked her would she be qualified to make such an observation and Aileen said she would not. Martin Kennedy asked her if she would be surprised to know that over thirty-two per cent of obstetricians who had not done a scan were surprised when a second baby came. Aileen said she accepted that.

Later in the Tribunal both Anthony and Martin Kennedy, trying to enhance the Twins Theory, called medical witnesses and invited and encouraged them to speculate on whether I had had twins, based solely on statistics such as my weight and height, my daughter Yvonne's weight at birth, the weights of my baby born on the farm and of the Caherciveen baby, regardless of the fact that none of these people had ever seen me during my pregnancy.

Jeremiah sat alone on the other side of the courtroom, surrounded by gardai but unaccompanied as he waited for the call to the witness stand. I felt sorry for him in his solitude. I had my friends all around me and he was utterly alone, pale and worried looking, fodder for the international press who had gathered to see and hear him.

We never glanced at one another or caught each other's eyes even for a moment. I heard them call his name and I watched him approach the chair. My God, we had shared so much in private! How far would he be expected to go in public? The sky was the limit as it transpired. The persecution process, through the clients of the Kennedys, would observe no standards of delicacy or compassion as long as they kept within the tenuous boundaries of the law. They would pound the media with sordid details that would capture the headlines of the world and delight the readers who didn't often get such real-life material from holy Ireland. Jeremiah Locke, the Daddy of them all, one magazine called him.

He told the Tribunal that he and his wife had two children, a boy born on 25 June 1982 and a girl born on 25 April 1984. He agreed that during both his wife's pregnancies I too had been pregnant by him. He accepted that he had been responsible for my three pregnancies. (He knew well that while I was involved with him there had been no other men in my life. Goodness knows, if there had been even the slightest chance of implicating anybody else the gardai would have produced him. Tom Flynn proved that.)

It hurt and surprised me to hear Jeremiah say that he had never intended leaving his wife to live with me. It hurt too when he revealed that I had not been a virgin when we first made love.

He described how our relationship had developed from initial friendship, when we would occasionally go for a drink, to an intimate sexual affair which involved making love in his car on a sideroad near my home. He agreed with Dermot McCarthy that my letter to Liam Bohan in which I had said that I really loved Jeremiah and not to be too hard on him was a true reflection of my feelings for him.

Later Martin Kennedy asked him if he loved me. He said he supposed he did.

"Is that your answer?"

"I did, yes."

"How much did you love her?"

"Depends on how you mean love. I was a married man."

"Do you accept you made Joanne pregnant at the same time as you made your wife pregnant?"

"I could not say. I am not an expert in that."

"You have fathered five children we know about and you say you are not an expert?"

"I don't know."

Martin Kennedy was again probing the sexual details of the affair. What had my lost virginity or the scene of our lovemaking to do with an investigation of garda behaviour? the letters to the newspapers asked. But the pattern continued. Kennedy wanted to know if it was Jeremiah or I who first suggested having sex. Jeremiah could not say. He supposed he pulled into the side of the road. Kennedy asked that an ordance survey map be shown to Jeremiah. He told him to point out where on the roadway between Tralee and Abbeydorney we used to stop.

Kennedy asked, "Who suggested that you drive down a side road?"

"Maybe she did," Jeremiah replied.

I was ready to scream.

The judge intervened. He wanted to know under which heading of the terms of reference this line of cross-examination was relevant. Kennedy said that if he could prove that "Joanne had a previous sexual history, which she did, and that at the time she had intercourse with this young man that she was also having intercourse with others and if one of those turns out to be blood group A it would be established that one of twins born as a result of that union could have A blood and the other O.''

Kennedy got the green light to proceed and he shot into overdrive. The Twins Theory had been launched.

"Your evidence is that you think it was she suggested it to you," he told Jeremiah.

"Well it takes two," Jeremiah replied.

Twice more Kennedy elicted the information that I had had sexual relations before I met Jeremiah. I couldn't believe my ears. What more did the man want to know? Was he expecting a revelation on the lines that a Kerry woman can lose her virginity more than once? Gone today, here tomorrow?

"And she may still be having sexual relations for all you know," he suggested.

Jeremiah replied that it was possible.

"Well, we know of one other," Kennedy said.

"Yes, but I don't know his name," Jeremiah replied.

"I will tell you his name. It's Tom Flynn."

"I never heard of the man."

Now I knew where I stood or, more accurately, tottered. The system was at work and I was fair game. All the sympathy and encouragement in the world wouldn't do now that the rules had been changed. Before my very eyes my own downfall was being enacted, my behaviour scrutinised in the name of the law so that the alleged improper conduct of the gardai could be investigated. This had nothing to do with interrogation methods or improper charges. This was a court of morals and I was on trial.

Jeremiah continued his story of our relationship and of his eight-hour stay at Tralee garda station. He told Kevin O'Higgins that during the questioning the pressure had been applied by Detective Sergeant O'Donnell and Detective Sergeant Downey. "They were trying to make me say I carried the baby to Caherciveen with Joanne," he told the Tribunal.

He said he had heard a scream in the station during the afternoon but he could not say whether it had come from a male or a female. He said it had frightened him and that a detective had told him it was nothing. "It passed my mind that it could have been Joanne Hayes but I did not ask the Guards who it was," he said.

Although he had signed his statement at around four o'clock he had not been allowed to go home, he told Dermot McCarthy "I would have gone home at two o'clock if I was let," he said. He insisted that he had asked earlier if he could go but that he was not allowed to leave until 8 p.m.

Jeremiah ended his evidence on day three of the Tribunal and did not attend again, but his troubles had not yet ended. In March he secured a court injunction against some personnel of the Thames Television programme *TV Eye,* claiming that he had been harassed by them at work in their effort to film him for a programme about the case.

Poor Jeremiah, for him 1985 has been a very bad year.

It was only a matter of time now, maybe a week my friends calculated as they trembled with me in anticipation of my call to the chair. When will you be on, I was asked time and again by people who sounded as if they were trying to plan their holidays to fit in the big event. Even the media could not resist joining in the guessing game, speculating on how long the remaining witnesses were likely to take and coming up with answers according to their calculations.

Meanwhile I listened to each witness and prayed that they would go on forever. Barry O'Halloran, the *Today Tonight* journalist, refused to disclose how copies of our written statements made in Tralee garda station became available to him. He confirmed that we had been paid basic fees of between £15 and £25 for our contributions to the programmes.

Elsie Moore recalled the contradictory stories I had told her about how far into my pregnancy I had been and that she had advised me to go to hospital straight away. Listening to her now I wished in my heart that I had told her the truth that night. She would have found my baby and insisted that everything would be brought out into the open. There would have been no Tribunal.

She told the relentless Martin Kennedy that the name of Tom Flynn meant nothing to her.

Mary Shanahan is a Tralee girl who is married to my first cousin Ted and lives about a mile from our house. She had been contacted by Garda Liam Moloney in his inquiries about my pregnancy. She had told him that I had lost the baby in hospital. She recalled visiting me in hospital and inquiring if I had life (was the baby alive?) and that I had replied that I had not. She had accompanied me to Dr Daly's surgery in Tralee on 13 April and told the Tribunal of my refusal to take the doctor's advice to go to hospital that night.

Having misled both these girls and also Dr Daly into believing that I had had a miscarriage I felt deeply ashamed now as I heard my catalogue of lies repeated in public.

John Falvey, Chief Education Officer in Tralee, whose Vocational Education Committee had overall responsibility for the sports centre, recalled his visit to Tralee garda station on the evening of 1 May to inquire about two of his staff who were being questioned there. He had called at about 8 o'clock. While he was standing in the reception area Jeremiah Locke was being escorted from the building. Jeremiah had seen Mr Falvey and had been embarrassed and the gardai had allowed him to leave by a side door. This little incident would assume greater significance at the Tribunal by establishing the exact time of Jeremiah's departure from the station.

Dr Harbison is a wild looking man with a shock of curly hair and an unruly beard that obscures most of his face. He is a David Bellamy lookalike, with a distinctive stoop when he walks. He has a strong polished voice and liked to illustrate his point with gestures from the witness box. On one occasion while giving evidence he searched the top pocket of his jacket for a biro and produced a toothbrush. Apart from being state pathologist, which involves him in the investigation of virtually every murder or suspicious death in the country, he is also lecturer in medical jurisprudence at Trinity College, Dublin.

Listening to Dr Harbison speak in clinical detail of his post mortem examinations was a gruesome experience. I didn't stay for much of it. "I was into the body before the full gravity of these marks was apparent to me," he said when explaining why he had gone ahead with the post mortem on the Caherciveen baby without a full back-up team. It had been his third post mortem that weekend.

He described the baby's injuries and said the stab wounds had been sustained in life. In his opinion the baby had not been stabbed in the mother's womb. "I would have had another victim on my hands with twenty-eight stab wounds through the abdominal wall," he explained. In his view a sharp pointed knife was the most likely weapon and from the enormous number of stab wounds he concluded there had been some degree of frenzy and panic. In his experience this most commonly involved the child's own mother. In cases of infanticide the child was killed while the mother was in a state of some derangement. It was most likely, but not necessarily, the mother who did it.

He had been surprised to see that the umbilical cord had been cut off flush with the skin. This had not been done medically and would be dangerous in a live birth because of the danger of bleeding and the need to have a margin to clamp it. The baby had been washed after birth.

Dr Harbison said that my baby had an umbilical cord of about thirty-six centimetres long. The left side of its neck and behind the left ear were discoloured and this may have been caused by bruising. The baby weighed over five pounds and there was evidence of fresh birth. Internal examination showed bleeding under the scalp surface. This may have been due to delivery, blows to the head or delivery on to a surface. There was a bruise on the left side of the neck but there was no injury to the larynx and this tended to exclude attempted strangulation.

He could not say whether my baby had attained a separate existence — whether it had survived at birth — other than to say that full expansion of the lungs had not taken place and that breathing had not been fully established but that did not preclude a separate existence. He could not give a cause of death and he had recorded it as unascertainabler. He had subsequently brought to Dublin some material including grass or hay which had been attached to the baby's body. He had asked that a search be made for a placenta but no placenta had been found. If a placenta (afterbirth) had been found it would have cleared up the question of whether twins had been involved, he said.

In court now our bathbrush was handed to him and he demonstrated the various uses it could have as a weapon. He said that if used to strike an infant on the head it would almost certainly have caused a fractured skull. Our carving knife was produced as an exhibit and he said he felt it was not the weapon which had caused the injuries to the Caherciveen baby because the knife would have caused a much longer opening.

By now the flowers and messages of support had started to arrive at home and at the Tribunal. The nation sensed blood and didn't like it. Ireland has a history of being the underdog and of being trampled by unsympathetic aggressors. Methaphorically speaking, history was being repeated.

In the courtroom itself history was being made as for the first time in his thirteen years as state pathologist Dr Harbison was being cross-examined by counsel for the gardai, not for clarification but for justification of his findings. The authorities had suddenly turned sceptical of their old ally. The first doubts concerned his memory. Anthony Kennedy said that at the post mortem on my baby many members of the Garda Siochana had been present and they had a clear recollection that at that time Dr Harbison had expressed the view that separate existence had been achieved.

Dr Harbison replied that he had been concerned about the bruises on the left side of the neck. He accepted that he may have stated at the post mortem that the baby had achieved separate existence; his final opinion was based on the microscopic appearance of the lung.

Anthony Kennedy put it to Dr Harbison that I had told a psychiatrist in Limerick that after giving birth I had panicked and killed the baby by putting my hands on its neck. He said he could not produce anything to corroborate that. (I felt a surge of elation at this news, overwhelming relief that I hadn't harmed my baby.) He said there were occasions when there was conflict between statements and findings and when he found such conflict he must confine himself to the findings.

He refused to state that one of the causes of death of my baby was abandonment in a field at night. It could be, but since he had not concluded on separate existence he had to leave that as a possibility.

Kennedy played his by now familiar sex card. "Is it possible that a man may have intercourse with a woman and deposit semen in her vagina and within ninety-six hours another man may have intercourse with the same woman and deposit semen in her vagina, and if that happened and there was a double ovulation that the woman could be impregnated in one ovum from the semen of the first man and in the other ovum by the semen of the other man?"

Dr Harbison said he could only speak having discussed it with experts in that field. It would be a very rare possibility, highly unlikely, according to the experts.

Dr Louise McKenna has worked in the National Forensic Science Department in Dublin for five years. She comes from Listowel, about twelve miles from Abbeydorney, and her father is a prominent businessman in the town. Slim and elegant and hardly thirty yet, she wears her expensive clothes with the casual confidence of the thorough specialist who has all the answers. If I was a disgrace to Abbeydorney she was a resounding credit to Listowel. Nobody disputed that she was the most impressive witness of the entire Tribunal.

Her evidence was highly technical but on her findings Jeremiah could be ruled out as the father of the Caherciveen baby, she said, but not of the baby born in Droumcunnig.

She said she had given information about the blood groupings to Superintendent Courtney in May. He had been surprised at the results and asked her if she was sure. They would not fit, she said. Superintendent Courtney had not asked her to do the tests again, nor did he suggest that she was wrong or say he did not accept the results. Anthony Kennedy asked her if she considered that her qualifications were sufficient to provide the expertise to analyse the tests. She replied that she had worked on muscles during her studies and had worked in the forensic science laboratory for five years. She dismissed the Bombay Gene theory as being so rare as not to be worthy of consideration. This theory had originated in India and shows that recessive genes hidden by more dominant blood types can exist. In other words, blood of a parent O grouping could, in fact, be hiding a weak A gene.

Martin Kennedy reminded Dr McKenna to state if questions she was asked were outside her field of expertise and added menacingly that there would be evidence on the questions he would ask. She again rejected the Bombay Gene proposition and told Mr Kennedy that she had asked colleagues to check her findings in some cases. They had been in agreement with her analysis. She told Kevin O'Higgins that the vegetation she saw was in the nature of hay. There was a significant amount of vegetation present on some of the samples she had received — these were the nightclothes I was wearing on the night of the birth.

Mr O'Higgins said that one of the suggestions was that I had given birth to a baby outdoors. Would her findings be consistent with that?

"It would, yes," Dr McKenna replied.

The hearings had been moved to the urban council chambers because the Circuit Court was sitting at the courthouse and now only three local doctors remained to be called before I faced the dreaded chair.

Dr Aidan Daly described my visit to him on the evening of 13 April and told of examining me and of the lies I had told to mislead him. He had been anxious to preserve the doctor-patient confidentiality between us when he was being interviewed by the gardai.

The doctor underwent a long and detailed cross-examination

during which he admitted making a wrong diagnosis but emphasised that he had been most anxious that I be hospitalised immediately and that he had recommended a scan. He had also told Elsie Moore that the police would have to be involved if my pregnancy had passed twenty-eight weeks.

Dr Aine O'Sullivan, who had been doing locum at St Catherine's Hospital, said she too had been misled by my story and had done a clinical examination. She had concluded that I was sixteen to eighteen weeks pregnant, pending the result of the scan. She said there had been a clampdown on information as there would be in any case because of doctor-patient confidentiality. Dr Creedon had told her he would deal with any questions.

Dr John Creedon, consultant obstetrician/gynaecologist, told of doing a scan and finding that I was not pregnant. After examining me he concluded that I had recently given birth to an at least advanced pregnancy. He had done a second scan as he was puzzled at the discrepancy between the history and the findings. Again nothing showed. He told of being interviewed by gardai subsequently and explained his difficult position in giving them the information they wanted. He recalled quoting cases he had seen before of patients coming to hospital with recent evidence suggestive of delivery and it had had a normal outcome. Cases of a similar nature in the past had been resolved. There had been a full discussion on the linking of the Caherciveen baby with me. He said there was no doubt that he had explained to the gardai that they could be on the wrong track and he was not surprised when my baby was found subsequently. He said the person responsible for the Caherciveen stabbings was insane and he did not think I was that kind of person.

He told Judge Lynch that it would not have been impossible for me to have delivered the baby on my own and it was also possible that I had had the baby in the yard, standing up. He said there would be a difference between an umbilical cord which was cut with an instrument and one which was torn.

Between them the doctors had given gynaecological details of my internal organs and menstrual records as a child might discuss the contents of a Christmas stocking. Parts of me that I never knew existed had been described and argued about before the public. I had abandoned any attempt to work out the connection between such information and an investigation of garda behaviour.

Giving Evidence

"THE DREADFUL HOURS of her ordeal upon the stand are now upon us," feminist and journalist Nell McCafferty wrote in the *Irish Press* of 16 January.

My head reeled as I fought the urge to be sick. The palms of my hands were sticky with sweat. It was 2.29 p.m. that day when my name was called.

My mother, my brothers and my sister were ordered to leave the courtroom. I was to suffer alone, or at least without those closest to me. I was terrified. I climbed on to the high chair and felt my legs dangling in the air. I was perched even higher than the judge. My God, the isolation! Michael Buckley, solicitor for the Tribunal, a kindly and ever helpful man, offered me a lower chair and I accepted gladly. Now my feet could touch the surface beneath me.

Michael Moriarty led me gently through my direct evidence about my background and my working career and my relationship with Jeremiah. I told of my miscarriage and the birth of Yvonne and the events of the night of 12/13 April in the field beside our house. I gulped water as I recalled these incidents and felt the pressure building up.

Giving evidence is a terrible experience. The natural inclination is to answer quickly so as to get on to the next question and the next. The quicker you answer the sooner it will be over! This, of course, is the worst thing a witness can do. Where it is necessary to elaborate you should do so but that's not how you see it when you are the target up there. You want to get out of the chair as quickly as possible and you throw away the opportunities to make valuable points. You feel that your troubles will be over as soon as you get down from that chair, not realising that what you have said will be repeated and interpreted and misinterpreted by the other side as it suits them.

It is only when you see the gardai in action that you realise that there is such a thing as an expert witness.

Mr Moriarty asked me what happened at Tralee garda station. I told about being taken upstairs to a big room and of Garda Moloney, our local garda in Abbeydorney, coming in. "I had known him for about six years. He asked me if I read *The Kerryman* and I said I did. He asked me if I had read about the Caherciveen baby and I said I had. He said 'That is your baby, Joanne,' and I said no it was not. Garda Moloney asked why had I denied about having had a baby and he said the baby in Caherciveen was mine. Then I told him about my own baby, but he did not believe me. He said my blood group and that of the Caherciveen baby matched.

"He asked me not to be covering up for anybody. He asked me was it Jeremiah Locke who got rid of the baby, or 'That oul' crowd from Fenit.' Jeremiah Locke's wife's people came from Fenit. . . .

"I told Garda Moloney I would take him out and show him exactly where the baby was in Droumcunnig. He continued to say I was covering up for somebody. Ban Gharda O'Regan made a cup of tea for me and Superintendent Courtney came in and stood in front of me and told me to tell the truth, because he knew who was involved and what we had done. He terrified me. He did not stay long, but he said he would be back and that I had better tell the truth.

"I was then alone with Garda Moloney and Ban Gharda O'Regan and I started to tell them about having had a baby on the night of the 12/13th. I told them I had a baby standing up, and that I broke the cord myself. Garda Moloney said that was impossible. Garda Moloney asked about where I put the baby and I explained very carefully where the baby was. He said, no, it was all lies. He told me the baby was out in Caherciveen.

"Ban Gharda O'Regan said it was impossible to have a baby standing up and to break the cord. Garda Moloney said I had everything rehearsed about what I was going to say, and I said it was the truth and I did have the baby."

"One detective said to call him by his Christian name and another by his initials. I was crying at that stage. . . . One of them was all about me at the start. He said it could be his own daughter that was in the room and that they didn't call murder of a baby murder any longer. It was called infanticide. They told me not to be crying and they said that if I told the truth I would not be put into jail, and all I needed was help.

"I gave them a full description again that I had the baby. I told the two detectives that I had the baby standing up and they did not believe me. They said the baby was buried in Caherciveen."

I told Mr Moriarty that the first statement I gave to Garda Moloney was the truth but that I didn't sign it. I said that the detectives seemed to believe me about my own baby, because I thought I heard one of them tell somebody to go out and get a search going.

I said, "I begged them to take me out to the exact spot, but they would not. One of them said he would not be made a fool of in front of his Inspector by a cheeky strap like me. He said he was going to bring the baby from Caherciveen and that I could identify it. They kept saying the Caherciveen baby was mine and I kept saying it was not.

"At one stage a detective brought in a notebook and read out a statement which he said my brother Ned had made. The statement said I had stabbed the baby in the chest. I can't remember anything else out of it, but I thought I was going to be sick, and I asked if I could go to the toilet, and one of the detectives put a newspaper on the floor and told me to get sick there, if I wanted to get sick. Later a detective let me go to the toilet.

"They kept at me to tell the truth. I kept asking them to take me to Abbeydorney. They they said that if I did not make a statement that they were going to charge Mom with murder as well, and that Yvonne would be put into an orphanage. One of them said I was a murderer. I said I was not.

"At that stage I think I told them I had killed my own baby. I asked them for a Bible and I would swear on the Bible that I was telling the truth. One of them said he would get a Bible, but it was never produced. They said the blood group of the Caherciveen baby matched my blood. They said that Kathleen was stupid and asked if she had done her Leaving Certificate and I said she had and one of them said you would never have known because she was so stupid.

"They said Ned had got rid of the baby. They said my mother was like a tramp on the side of the road and that they knew my aunt and that she was a nurse and it was unknown how many people we had killed between the two of us. They said Michael would not milk a cow for a long time.

"Around this time Detective Officer Coote and Detective Officer Smith came in. They had a carving knife and a white bathbrush and a turf bag. They asked me did I recognise these items and I said I did because they belonged to us. Detective Officer Coote then read out a statement by my mother. The statement was that I had given birth to a baby in my bedroom, and that I got a bath brush and beat the baby with it and stabbed the baby, and that my brothers, Ned and Michael, took the baby, and I am not sure if Dingle was mentioned or not.

"I told the detectives I could not remember anything of that and one of them said I had probably blacked out. I said I would surely remember if I had stabbed a baby. Some of the detectives were roaring and shouting at this time. One kept imitating me. Everything I would say, he would say."

Mr Moriarty asked me if at some stage something happened that made me change my mind. I told him that the gardai again told me that my mother would be charged with murder and Yvonne would be put into an orphanage and that the farm would be sold that evening. "I was crying all the time and it was at this stage that they left the room and that Garda Moloney came in. I had no idea of the time. I drew a map of the spot where the baby was for Garda Moloney. I told Garda Moloney that I would make a statement, but it was not going to be the truth. He said he could not take the statement then. He told me to tell the truth, because the crowd from Dublin would only be roaring and shouting.

"I told him I would give the statement they wanted, but it was not going to be the truth. I did not want the lads to be charged with murder and Yvonne to be put in an orphanage, but he said he could not take the statement like that. I told him to send in the two Dublin fellows and they would take it. Garda Moloney asked how would I remember all the statement that was read out to me, and I said I would remember bits and make up the rest.

"I think one of the detectives asked Garda Moloney if I was telling the truth and Garda Moloney said I was telling the truth. Garda Moloney left and one of the detectives was writing the statement. They were still roaring. One detective was saying most of the statement. He would say such things as 'you got the knife', and I said 'ya', and he would say 'where did you get the knife?' and I would say 'in the kitchen'. He asked me where did I get the bathbrush and I said in the bathroom. He asked me how did I stab the baby and I said 'in the back'. He was putting everything to me and I was agreeing and another detective was writing down the statement.

"They asked me was I sorry. I said 'yes'. They asked me was I ashamed. They seemed to be delighted. They told me not to be sayin 'ya' every minute and to say out my statement."

I told Mr Moriarty that I was not sure if they read out the statement. They had asked me to sign it and I did. He asked me what was the state of my mind at the time and I told him I was crying and that I didn't think my mind was my own. He asked if my statement concluded with an expression of my being sorry and I told him that that was the idea of one of the detectives.

I told Mr Moriarty about being taken downstairs to see my aunt, Bridie Fuller, in another room. "I told her to tell them that I had killed the baby, because she would not be let out of there that night if she didn't tell them."

I told Mr Moriarty about the brief hearing at which I was charged by Sergeant Dillon and of being taken downstairs afterwards where I met members of my family. I told him that Kathleen said her statement was all lies, and that I had said, "the same here", and that I told Kathleen to go down the field the following day and told her where I had put the baby.

I told him of being kept in a cell during the night and of being charged with murder at Tralee District Court the following day. "I don't know why I pleaded guilty to the charge," I told Mr Moriarty. "I had not slept the previous night."

Mr Moriarty asked if I had said anything by way of complaint about what had been done to me and I said "no".

That first afternoon in the chair had been relatively easy, Mr Moriarty had been kind and undersanding with me when I became upset as some particularly unpleasant memories were stirred up but it was my own emotions rather than pressure from the floor that brought the tears.

I cried again several times the next day as Mr Moriarty and my own counsel Dermot McCarthy took me back through the catalogue of love and pain and misery and anguish that had landed me before them.

Mr Moriarty asked whether at any stage I had said "I am a murderess, I killed my baby," and replied that one of the detectives had kept shouting at me and told me to say it and in the end I did. I thought this was after he had read out the statement that Ned was supposed to have made in which he said I had stabbed the baby in the chest.

I swore to the Tribunal that it was my true evidence that there was never any question of my having had twins. "After I had started my relationship with Jeremiah Locke there was never any other man in my life," I said.

Did I know anybody called Tom Flynn, asked Dermot McCarthy, my own senior counsel. No. No, I hadn't been a virgin when Jeremiah Locke and I had first made love and, yes, it was silly and stupid not to have told my family about my pregnancy and not to have gone to a doctor. The reason I hadn't applied for maternity leave was that I had no intention of going back to work afterwards. I had intended getting a flat in Tralee for myself and my two children.

Yes I had heard Dr Harbison say that in his opinion the umbilical cord had been cut but he was wrong. I had pulled it and it had broken. I had been terrified of Dr Daly's mention of the police because I had abandoned my baby and I was afraid they would find me out. I had thought I would be put in jail. That was why I hadn't told him the full story.

How had I felt when I heard about the Caherciveen baby? I had felt terrible but I knew it wasn't my baby. I had abandoned my baby, the Caherciveen baby had been murdered.

"Why did you admit to stabbing the Caherciveen baby?" Dermot asked.

"They kept roaring and shouting at me to tell them that I had stabbed the baby and in the end I was convinced I had done it," I replied. I was crying bitterly now at the memory of that night in the station.

"If you could get the family off the hook and give the gardai the Caherciveen baby when they could not find the other baby you would be quite happy to admit to one as the other?" Dermot asked.

I said, "I was not happy about it at all but it seemed to satisfy them."

The inquiry was very stressful for me. Was the stressful feeling the same as I experienced at the garda station, Dermot asked. "No, I think garda stations have a different effect on people. You are not roaring and shouting at me here," I replied.

I blessed myself and asked Mary, Mother of God, to help me as Anthony Kennedy, SC, stood up. I hadn't been able to eat the meals that Auntie Aquinas cooked for us and I had endured several sleepless nights in anticipation of this moment. He looked straight at me over the top of his spectacles, removed them for an instant with the tips of two fingers, then put them on again and began in the cultivated accent that amused so many of his fellow townspeople. "Miss Hayes"; the words seemed to come through his nose rather than from his mouth. I heard them hundreds of times in my nightmares during the subsequent months. You wouldn't think it now but he was an ex-pupil of my old convent school at Moyderwell.

I gulped down water at every chance and told myself that I must concentrate.

I sobbed as Kennedy recalled the entry of the detectives into the interrogation. Yes, I had denied giving birth and I had told them that I had a miscarriage and had flushed it down the toilet. I remember O'Carroll saying that it would be in the septic tank so. No, I had not broken down at that stage and confessed to killing my own baby. I probably had described the birth in detail but I did not remember telling them.

I agreed with Mr Kennedy that Dr Fennelly had not been harassing me and was a sympathetic doctor trying to treat me. I agreed I had told him about having the baby in the field and panicking. Kennedy said that I had told Dr Fennelly that when I had the baby I had killed it by putting my hand on its throat. "If he says I said it, I probably did," I cried. Kennedy said I had told Detectives O'Carroll and Browne that the baby had been crying but that I had not said this to Dr Fennelly.

I replied that as far as I knew the baby had not cried. "Why would I be charged with the murder of the Caherciveen baby and not my own?" I cried again.

The gardai made more requests to me to tell the truth, Mr Kennedy suggested, "I don't know was it requests," I replied.

I agreed with Mr Kennedy that the question of the farm being sold that evening did not sound credible.

"They say that was never said."

"It was; at that stage I would have believed anything."

Kennedy suggested that during the taking of the statement I had come towards one of the detectives crying and had leant against him and that as I clung to him he had put his arms around me.

I had made no complaint to Aunt Bridie, he said. "She did not understand what was going on," I replied.

I could not remember Kathleen's reaction when I told her about the child after being charged. Up until then nobody had known what had happened in the field. Kathleen had not cut the cord.

I didn't know how it came to have a sharp cut on it. "I broke it, that is all I can say," I sobbed.

The pressure was getting to me now. I was only too aware of how lonely it had been and reliving it now in public was too much for me. I had no control over the tears that flowed. Dermot McCarthy, SC, asked the judge to allow time for me to compose myself.

"It would not be helpful one way or another. Proceed," the judge ordered.

Once more I tried to tell them about the birth, the panic, the aftermath. I was sobbing as I spoke. Dermot McCarthy again asked the judge to allow me time to compose myself.

"We will pause," the judge said authoritatively.

A minute later I was telling Anthony Kennedy that I didn't know how long the panic had lasted. I had not been delirious but the panic had been pretty intense. Yes I had been weak when it was all over and I had had to cross a sort of ditch to get to the place where I had put the baby but I had not found it difficult. No I had not got special clothes for the child. Yvonne's clothes would do.

When had I made love first, Mr Kennedy asked. About four our five years ago, I said.

"I understand it was quite a long period between that happening and you going out with Jeremiah Locke."

"I went out with Jeremiah Locke in 1981."

"How long before that was it that you had had sex with somebody else?"

"About a year. It did not happen many times with that other person."

At last Anthony Kennedy sat down. My tears were of relief now. The judge was speaking. I looked at Kennedy who was on his feet again. Had he ever done what we would consider a decent day's work, I asked myself, like getting his hands dirty, or had he ever got drunk or ever let a four-letter word escape those lips? Was he really whiter than white?

The judge was saying that it had been put to other witnesses that I had had twins and that it had not been put to me. Kennedy said he thought it had been put to me by another counsel.

"I want to know what your case is," said Judge Lynch.

Kennedy turned to me once more. Had I had twins? No, I had not, I replied.

"I must suggest to you that that is what happened, that you had a baby born outside and then a baby born in the house some two hours or so afterwards."

"I don't agree with that."

"And that for whatever reason, you did what is described in these statements."

"No."

"Probably in some state of panic or frenzy because you never expected the second child to come."

"No. There was only one child."

"And without going into the statement again that what that describes is broadly the truth of what happened on that night in your house."

"No."

"And that since then you have persisted in a denial and disowning these statement, that it has become exaggerated with the passage of time by adding to the complaints against the gardai."

"No, I don't agree."

He sat down again. Those final questions had been fired like bullets and I was exhausted. Judge Lynch gave me the option of continuing in the witness box or resuming in the morning. Martin Kennedy was straining at the leash. You must be joking, I thought to myself. I said I would prefer to start next morning. The judge said it would be better if I didn't consult with my legal advisers overnight.

Martin Kennedy and I had got off to a bad start. Early in the Tribunal he had persistently referred to me as Joanna or Johanna, names that I absolutely hate being called, and I had asked Brian Curtin to correct him. Now, as I waited to take my seat on the chair again, I watched him fiddling with the papers that were stacked in front of him. I had received several bouquets and four dozen single flowers on arrival at the urban council offices that morning but such visible support did nothing to ease my helplessness.

Dermot McCarthy said he wanted to raise a matter arising from Anthony Kennedy's cross-examination of the previous day. He said Mr Kennedy had not put it to me that I had had twins until after it had been mentioned by the judge. It had been put on the basis that it was twins and not on the basis that it was twins by different fathers. As Dermot McCarthy understood it the case which was being made for several days by both Kennedy's, on behalf of the gardai, was that they were endeavouring to counter the evidence of Dr McKenna and putting forward a certain extreme theory which had been set out by Mr Martin Kennedy on day three.

Dermot said: "Mr Kennedy told your Lordship that if he could establish that she was having a sexual relationship with some other men other than Mr Locke and that if the blood group of this other peson turned out to be blood group A then he was going to produce evidence to show that twins could be born with different fathers and the twins would have different blood groups. No such evidence had yet been produced to the Tribunal."

He said one would also be expecting evidence relating to the "alternative father". He had not received any proof or statement of any witnesses they intended calling.

The judge said he was not overlooking the fact that the evidence had not been produced. He said that they might not wish to call any witnesses and they might rely on the evidence of the doctor who agreed that it was a possibility. They were entitled to rely on such evidence as was elicited in cross-examination.

Martin Kennedy is a big and loud man. Described in one of the papers as a devout Catholic he is chairman of a branch of Fianna Fail, the political party to which I and all my family belong. Beside him as his junior sat Brendan Grogan, whose father had for years been Supreme Knight of the Knights of Columbanus, the Roman Catholic equivalent of the Protestant Freemason Society. If my own priests weren't behind me the opposition had a distinctly religious backbone.

Kennedy went straight into the attack. He reminded me of what the judge had said about not consulting with my legal advisors overnight and wondered what I had been discussing with Mr Mann in room thirteen after the previous day's hearing.

I said I had been discussing his suit.

"Whose suit?"

"Mr Mann's."

I said we had also discussed Mr Mann's overcoat but we had not talked about the case.

The public laughed at this exchange but what I had said was absolutely true. There had been several people in room thirteen and Aileen Enright's sister Mary had made tea for us as she did every day. Somebody had pointed out to Patrick Mann that there was a button missing from his overcoat and somebody else had said it was about time he changed his suit. Whether it was as a result of that observation or not Patrick bought himself three new suits a week later.

Mr Kennedy wanted to establish that I was a liar. I said I didn't find it difficult to distinguish between truth and untruth. I agreed that it was possible that lies came easy to me when they suited my purpose. He detailed the series of lies I had told my friends prior to the birth of my baby.

Then, his two hands leaning heavily on the table in front of him as if he were fighting an impulse to leap at me, he asked why I had given the Tribunal an untrue account of the birth of my baby outside the house. I asked him what he meant. He repeated the question and I said I had not given an untrue account.

Had I been intimate with Jeremiah Locke on the first occasion that he drove me home? Yes, I said, it just happened. Kennedy said these things don't just happen, they require the consent of two people. I agreed that maybe my love for Jeremiah had been a one-sided love. Did I accept that my expressed hope to live happy ever after with him was only in fairy tales, like a prince finding a princess and putting her up onto his white charger and riding off into the sunset. I said I realised that that hope would not be fulfilled after Yvonne was born. Yes, I still loved Jeremiah. He had said that he was in love with me and I had asked him why he didn't come to live with me. He had said he would eventually.

Yes, I was upset that he appeared to show no interest in Yvonne. I had continued to associate with him because I still loved him. Yes, even after the birth of Yvonne. So, was I hoping to use my daughter as ammunition to force Jeremiah to leave his wife and child and come and live with me? No, I did not have the baby for him, I had it for myself.

Was I still continuing to associate with Jeremiah? No, I had been out with him last a good bit before 12 April and I had not been intimate with him then.

Kennedy asserted that while I was out working and enjoying myself Kathleen was staying at home minding the baby. I told him that Kathleen went out regularly as well. When she went out at night I stayed at home. I paid Kathleen £20 a week. I earned £88 and gave £30 at home for my keep.

"Do you think Kathleen was happy with that arrangement?"

"I cannot say. You will have to ask her."

"Would you tell us the circumstances of your miscarriage on

the Bank Holiday of June 1982? I am not intruding in your privacy."

"Aren't you?"

He said that the suggestion would be made that I transposed in my mind what happened then with what happened in 1984. I said I was at work and I had felt blood going down my leg. I had gone into the toilet and had passed one big clot. He asked about the row that occurred with relatives of Jeremiah when they were waiting near my house. I told him that they had pulled me out of Jeremiah's car.

"Did they accuse you of anything?"

"They probably did, yes. I can't remember."

He said I had a very convenient memory. There were certain things I could remember and certain things I couldn't remember at all.

I said Jeremiah had followed me down the road and we had stayed at a friend's house that night. I agreed that on that occasion Jeremiah had chosen his girl friend. I said he had gone back to his wife next day.

How had we got together again? I could not say.

"Now, Miss Hayes, please. You had a very unpleasant row. One of these ladies had pulled you out of the car. Your relationship came to an end and the Tribunal would like to know why and how the relationship resumed."

"He probably drove me home."

"On your suggestion?"

"I can't say."

"Or you won't say?"

"I can't say."

I said I had been delighted when I had become pregnant in August 1982 but my family had been upset.

"But your attitude was not the same when it came to your next pregnancy."

"Yes."

"You had no intentions of allowing that child to be alive in this world after it left your body."

"That's untrue."

"And that is the reason why you did not tell your doctor, your nurse or apply for thirteen weeks maternity leave. Is that the reason?"

"No."

"And that is the reason you went out that night, that terrible night, Thursday 12 April 1984, and delivered yourself of that baby in the open field."

"No, it's not true."

I became very upset and Kennedy paused before continuing. Somebody said afterwards that I sounded like a banshee in the otherwise silent courtroom.

He referred back to the Christmas party. Yes, I had been very annoyed at hearing that Jeremiah's wife was pregnant. Jeremiah had shown no concern for myself or the unborn baby and, no, he had not asked about adoption or abortion. We had never been intimate after that night. Jeremiah had told me at the start of the relationship that he was not getting on with his wife. I had never said that I didn't want the baby. I wanted the baby.

"When you wanted Yvonne you sought medical advice. Why did you not do this when you were expecting this baby?"

"I don't know."

"The only reason open to you, Miss Hayes, is that you did not want that baby."

"That is not true."

"And what did you do to show that you wanted the baby?"

"Nothing."

"Nothing."

Again he had to pause while I cried.

Now I had aspirations that this would end soon.

Why had I told Dr Fennelly that I had had the baby in the field and panicked, killing the child by putting my hands on his neck? I replied I had pulled the baby on the neck when I was pulling him out.

"Did you not realise you were killing your baby?"

"No."

"Well, you knew you were not doing him any good."

"I did not know what I was doing."

He paused again while I sobbed. The pause was not of compassion but to get me ready to take more. I felt like vomiting. Surely no woman lawyer would condone such cruelty. Where were the women lawyers? Was there no place for them?

"You knew that the baby, even if it was then alive, could not have survived a night in the open unattended?"

"Yes."

I said again that I had pulled the umbilical cord and that it broke.

I did not know what way it broke and I had continued to bleed after the birth. Kennedy said that where bleeding mostly occurred was when the cervix of the womb was not closed because there was a second child there. I said I had had only one child.

"At half past two you suddenly realised after you thought all your troubles were over here was another to come."

"No, there was only one baby."

He said that I had called Aunt Bridie who had great difficulty before the child was born "and in your terrible state you got the knife and stabbed the baby as described in your statement".

"That is all untrue."

"Not only were you stabbing the baby, you beat that baby with a bathbrush as shown to the Tribunal by Dr Harbison."

"That is not my baby."

"Was there another baby born in that house?"

"No. That baby out in Caherciveen was not mine." (Oh God, I prayed, by some miracle let the real mother come forward!)

"If you say it was not yours can you say whose it is?"

"No." (How I wished I could.)

He said Kathleen knew all about it because she was present when the baby was born and that it was in fact Kathleen who disposed of the baby. I said "no". Who pulled the cord? I pulled the cord. Why hadn't I told that I had the baby? I was afraid. Of whom? The gardai.

"You had done no wrong. You were going to have a baby and you go into a field because you had no alternative. What had you done wrong?"

"I don't know what I had done. I knew I had given birth to a child and I didn't know if I had harmed the child or not."

"How could you have harmed it?"

"I abandoned it."

"Yes. It was a dead baby. It's no crime to abandon a dead baby."

"I thought it was."

The judge pointed out that as a matter of law it was a crime to conceal birth.

"You were in hospital for a week and you were back home without a baby. Do you expect the Tribunal to believe that, do you?"

"There was no mention of the baby."

He referred to the day I was taken to the station in Tralee. I said I was asked to go; I did not offer to go. I could not say how long I was with Garda Moloney in the station.

I said Detective Superintendent Courtney had stayed less than ten minutes in the room.

"A detective will say that he did not say it and nobody said it in his presence that he would not be made a fool of by a cheeky strap like you."

I said he had said that and that he had also said he would bring in the baby and I could identify him.

"He will say there's no truth in that and that it is a figment of your fertile imagination."

"He said it. I said I would not like to see a dead baby."

"Did you not see a dead baby on the morning of 13 April?"

"Yes."

"What is wrong with seeing another one?"

"It was not mine."

Kennedy asked about what he called the kernel of the case. "One of the detectives said you were a murderer. You said you were not. You said it was now a lot less friendly."

"Yes."

Kennedy asked about the sketch I claimed to have given to Garda Moloney. I said he had supplied the paper, a big sheet of paper with no lines on it. I had drawn a sketch of the spot where I had put the baby.

"Garda Moloney went off with this non-existent sketch?"

"There was a sketch."

The hearing adjourned until Monday and I was left facing a terrible weekend. Some of my friends persuaded me to go for a few drinks that Friday night and everybody kept telling me not to worry, that I wasn't on trial. I was like a wasp at home, snapping at everybody for no reason and all the time dreading the resumption of my encounter with the devout Catholic on Monday. I never slept that weekend.

Again the flowers and letters of sympathy and support arrived as people resented what the press called "Womanhood on Trial".

Martin Kennedy stood in his familiar pose and looked straight into my eyes. I stared back at him. Why, if the detectives had treated me so badly had I asked for them when I agreed to give a statement? At that stage it was all the same, I said. I was not going to tell the truth anyway.

Once more he took me through the confession, suggesting that it was all true while I denied each accusation. I was very tired and soon I became distraught again as we went over the same heartbreaking ground.

Dermot McCarthy asked for a break as I was under stress. Judge Lynch said I would be under stress all morning. I would have to do the best I could.

I had very little fight or energy left and began to give answers like "If they say so", "I presume so", "I suppose so". Kennedy said I either remembered or not. He didn't want any more supposes. He referred to "so much gratuitous detail" in my statement and I said it was there because the detectives kept asking me questions.

I repeatedly denied having had twins and as Dermot McCarthy again intervened I asked the judge if I could go out. Judge Lynch agreed and I ran crying loudly from the courtroom. I got sick outside the door and had several bouts of empty vomiting while my friends who had followed me wept in sympathy with me. One of them phoned Dr Joe Arthurs and he arrived very quickly and tried to treat me while I screamed that I wasn't going to go back to the court. He gave me tablets and told me to relax but I was very excited and frightened.

Dr Arthurs was called to give evidence about my condition when the Tribunal resumed almost an hour later. He said that I was hyperventilating, that I was nauseous and that I had got sick once in his presence. My pulse was fast and I was showing signs of acute anxiety. I was shaking and unable to communicate and my pulse rate was 120. Dermot McCarthy asked if in his opinion I was fit to take the stand again.

"Certainly not," Dr Arthurs replied. He said that a person suffering from acute anxiety would have to be given sedation. He did not think I would be able to answer questions. Asked whether the fact that I had been given sedation would make it difficult for me to give evidence he said it was a difficult question to answer.

Sedation had different effects on different people. He said there was a reasonable possibility that I would be able to give evidence at 2.15 p.m. He also said that I had told him that I had not been getting much sleep.

Michael Moriarty said it would appear that nothing would be gained by putting me back to the following day. Dr Arthurs replied that from a medical point of view it would be better. Judge Lynch asked the doctor which would be better, sooner or later. Dr Arthurs said that I needed some time but if I responded to sedation I might be able to give evidence in the afternoon. Judge Lynch said it seemed that the weekend break had done me no good. Dr Arthurs said he was not sure what I had been through that morning and could not say what had precipitated my condition.

While they discussed my capacity to take further punishment, in terms of when rather than if, just as somebody would ask a mechanic when the car would be ready, I was fighting the sense of panic and hysteria that had virtually broken me.

"Don't give in to the bastards; don't let them get the better of you," was the theme in that room and I don't mind admitting that the air was fairly blue. Kathleen had been called when it was decided that I wasn't fit to resume immediately. With legal costs at around £4,000 per day the show must go on. Meanwhile my mother and the rest of my family would watch the doctor recharge my battery.

I made up my mind that I would face the devout Catholic again after lunch. It might as well be sooner rather than later; I was on the way out anyway. Dr Arthurs testified that I was fit to give evidence and I took the chair once more.

The judge had some consoling words for me. He said that in due course every one of the gardai mentioned would have to go into the witness box and be subjected to cross-examination as hard as my counsel saw fit. Sex lives and all, I wondered, or would they draw the line at sadistic tendencies? Judge Lynch said counsel for the gardai was entitled to test the allegations made.

"My function is to try to get at the truth. My duty is to sit here and listen. I want you to try and complete your evidence but you have to put up with strenuous cross-examination," he said.

So, "strenuous" was the word for it. Hundreds of people around the country had different views and adjectives for the Kennedy approach.

Kennedy continued to take me through my incriminating statement. Was it my evidence that two of the detectives had concocted my statement? Yes it was. Why did I say Aunt Bridie did not know what was going on? Because she asked me what was going on.

He asked me why I had said "I am guilty" when I was charged and I said I had been convinced that I had done it.

"Who convinced you that you had done it?"

"Two of the detectives. They kept telling me I did it. I told them I was not guilty."

Kennedy asked me if someone kept telling me that it was raining outside when I knew it was not would I believe it.

"You would if it was in Tralee garda station."

The judge asked at the conclusion of the day's hearing how long more Mr Kennedy expected the cross-examination to last. Kennedy said he hoped to finish next day but it could go into the following day.

I nearly fell off the chair. I had completed my fourth day's evidence and still there was no indication of an impending finish. I have never felt worse in my life than I did that evening. Mary O'Riordan insisted that I stay with her that night. I took my sleeping tablet early and shortly afterwards wanted to go for a walk. "No way," Mary almost screamed at me. A night's sleep would be vital.

Next morning I had serious doubts that I could take any more. The girls showed me the stacks of flowers and the letters that had arrived. I had taken the prescribed sedatives so that I could come under the judge's orders. They had succeeded in getting me to the chair, ready if neither willing nor able. Afterwards it was reported that my voice was noticeably slurred.

Several times I told Kennedy that I could not remember volunteering a statement to Ban Gharda O'Regan and Detective Garda Brew without being asked any questions. The judge asked if there would be evidence that Ban Gharda O'Regan and Detective Brew had not asked any questions. Kennedy said that as far as he knew there hadn't been an interview for the purpose of taking a statement. Judge Lynch said he wanted to know everybody's case at every stage. Dermot McCarthy pointed out that Kennedy was appearing for three superintendents and not for the gardai. Martin Kennedy had stumbled, tripped up by his own enthusiasm. Lawyers on £400 a day could afford such slips. It would be different for a witness.

Kennedy wanted to know about Tom Flynn. I said I did not

know anybody of that name or how his name came to be written in blue biro on the mattress taken from our home.

How many boyfriends had I before I met Jeremiah Locke? One. And after Jeremiah? None. Kennedy claimed that I continued to associate with my first boyfriend or commenced a new association with somebody else while I was going out with Jeremiah. He said that around August 1983 I had been intimate with some man other than Jeremiah.

"No. That is not true," I said.

He said that as well as being intimate with Jeremiah at the time I had also been intimate with another man within the space of forty-eight hours.

"That's not true," I said again.

He said that the reason I had not gone to a doctor was because I had no interest in the safety or well-being of the baby. It had been a considered failure on my part to take the steps necessary for my own good.

I tried to say no but I don't think the word came out.

Had I never been tempted to seek medical help? "No, I don't know," I replied. (I felt that I was about to collapse). Why not? I don't know.

I was unable to communicate now; the tears had taken over. I was past caring what happened.

Dermot McCarthy asked the judge to allow me a few minutes to compose myself. Judge Lynch told me I could step down. He was wondering whether it would be better to continue and be finished or to drag on and on. I was on my way out the door.

It is possible to run out of tears. I would cry hysterically for a few minutes in our room until I somehow crashed some kind of barrier and then I would dry up. No more tears, just a choking feeling and a thumping in the chest that would eventually subside. Outwardly I would be calm and composed again. My pale complexion was normal; the inner wounds didn't show.

Ten minutes later Kennedy was back on the attack. "Is it not true that you did not want this baby?"

"It is not true," I replied.

On the day that I was brought from the sports centre was it not obvious to me that they had wanted to talk to me about the Caherciveen baby? "You were pregnant; it was widely known. You were now no longer pregnant. It was obvious you had had one or more babies," he said.

"I had one baby," I replied.

The death of the Caherciveen baby had made headlines. "And you are swearing that it never crossed your mind that you might be a suspect?"

"It never dawned on me."

I said I could offer no reason why wild animals had not interfered with the baby during the two and a half weeks before gardai took it away. I denied that the reason was that it had been put there after the gardai had searched the area.

He said that I had spent a lot of money on clothes after the charges had been dropped and said I had been paid or bribed into giving interviews to the media. I replied that I had received a once-off payment of £300 as a PRSI (tax) refund. I had received £25 for the television interviews and had got nothing from the newspapers.

And then it was over. The devout and learned counsel had asked 2,216 questions and now he sat down.

Kevin O'Higgins was mercifully polite and brief. I told him that in the entire period that I had spent in the garda station nobody had suggested to me that I had had twins. He asked me to draw a sketch similar to the one I had drawn for Garda Moloney.

I agreed with Mr O'Higgins that I had been feeling ashamed and sorry for what I had done in relation to my own baby. He quoted from my letter to Liam Bohan and I agreed with his interpretation that I had been feeling guilty and ashamed about my own baby. I also agreed that I did not know if my baby had been alive when born and that in those circumstances I had felt very ashamed and guilty as the mother of a newborn baby.

Had that guilt and remorse been to the forefront of my mind going into Tralee station that day? Yes, I replied.

Had I any plans about the parcel on the farm had the gardai not come? I said I would have had to tell somebody.

The judge said I would have to be weighed and measured and that he would want Dr Creedon back to give evidence again. He smiled and thanked me and I paused in case anybody else had any ammunition left and then I thanked the judge and walked out of the room. It was 12.35 p.m. Kennedy had finished much earlier than he had forecast. I will always believe that that forecast was a deliberate attempt to put even more pressure on me overnight and that he knew well that he would finish when he did.

Inside the judge ordered that a photograph be taken of the exact

Demonstration on 23 January. (Derek Speirs/Report)

Escort through the demonstration: Sergeant Terry Cronin, Detective Garda Con O'Sullivan, Detective Garda Tim O'Callaghan; Detective Garda Michael Smith; Judge Kevin Lynch, Sergeant Michael Coote. (Michael MacSweeney).

spot on the farm where my baby had been found. He also asked that a rugby ball be put into the plastic bag in which my baby had been found and that it be photographed in the position where the baby had been located. He also ordered that photographs of the bags in which the chemist's bag was found be taken and produced for the Tribunal.

I drank mugs of tea and tried to share my friends' delight that my ordeal was over, but so much was yet to come. Kathleen was now in the box and the rest of the family would have to sweat it out until their turns came. I was totally disillusioned with everything the Tribunal stood for.

My neighbours in Abbeydorney decided that the time had come when they should stand up and be counted. Country people don't like to pry so they had stayed away from the Tribunal deliberately, but they shared the sense of outrage that had gripped the counry. Completely unknown to any of my family the parish was about to display its heart.

On the morning of 23 January sixty-six Abbeydorney people marched outside the Tribunal building carrying placards which read "Abbeydorney Supports Joanne". They had left their farms, their kitchens, their jobs and had defied the worst road conditions of the year to make their gesture. The group was equally divided between men and women. For more than an hour they paraded, explaining to the astonished media that they had no wish to be in contempt of the Tribunal but that they felt that we should not be allowed to suffer alone. Some were severely critical of the direction that the cross-examination on behalf of the gardai had taken.

Many of the marchers could only spare a few minutes off from their jobs but they turned up to show their solidarity. I arrived alone that morning and my heart jumped as I saw my friends on parade. Some of them rushed forward to shake my hand and to tell me to keep the spirit up. This was above politics or any other motivation except compassionate good neighbourliness.

According to prominent feminist Nell McCafferty it was an historic occasion because it was the first time Irish men had marched in support of an unmarried mother. All I know is that it was a gesture that I will never forget. It was a tremendous boost to our morale and a public rebuff to certain individuals who watched from inside the windows of the building.

On the following Friday night on *The Women's Programme* on

television Nell McCafferty saluted the men of Abbeydorney as she had promised by adding "Goodnight Brothers" to her customary "Goodnight Sisters" at the end of her slot.

Next day the Tralee Women's Action Group staged a demonstration outside the Tribunal and they too were supported by quite a number of men. Women had defied terrible road conditions to travel from as far as Dublin and Cork and they made their feelings known in no uncertain terms as some of the legal figures emerged at the end of the day's hearing. I was dismayed to hear that Judge Lynch had received a hostile reception and that it had been deemed necessary to give him a garda escort to his hotel, but neither I nor any of my family had had anything to do with organising the protest and we had no control over what was done.

At the next hearing Judge Lynch warned that anyone attempting to frustrate or interfere with the proceedings could face a jail sentence of two years and or fines of up to £10,000. He said he would not tolerate any further demonstrations, even silent and peaceful ones, within the precincts of the Tribunal. He would use his extensive powers as a High Court judge to protect the independence and integrity of the Tribunal. He also said that those who had attacked the cross-examination of witnesses should know better.

Only persons with access to the files and documents, he said, could appreciate what may or may not be relevant. Other persons having no such access who declared that the Tribunal was straying outside its terms of reference did not speak from the founts of wisdom and knowledge.

He said that Patrick Mann had acted entirely correctly and properly in advising us not to go forward for questioning at the internal garda inquiry because if it turned out that we might have been charged with offences relating to my baby he would have been failing gravely in his duty to protect our interests. But, he added, it would be monstrous if those who now stood accused by the only subsisting allegations in the inquiry — the gardai — were not to be allowed to defend themselves as strongly as possible, "including strenuous cross-examination of the Hayes family".

He said that, in fairness to the people of Abbeydorney, the silent and dignified protest organised by the people of rural Ireland was in marked contrast to the raucous assembly on Thursday, gathered from the four corners of urban Ireland. He believed that our family did not instigate the demonstrations. It would be a matter for the

Director of Public prosecutions to decide whether he wished to take proceedings against those responsible. At the same time it was likely, he said, that the Director of Public Prosecutions would bear in mind that those responsible for the demonstrations might have been misled by individual members of the Dail and Seanad whose utterances had been given wide publicity earlier the previous week.

He had not asked for an escort when leaving the courthouse but the garda authorities, in view of the situation, had decided to provide one. That was perfectly proper but he was somewhat concerned to see that some of the persons involved in the escort were gardai involved in the Tribunal. If any such escort became necessary again he wished to make it clear that it should not involve any gardai involved in the Tribunal proceedings.

Judge Lynch spoke for half an hour and after he concluded Dermot McCarthy said he wished to emphasise that we did not in any way prompt, suggest or originate the protests. We had no hand, act or part in them, he said. The judge said he fully accepted that.

As Judge Lynch was addressing the Tribunal in Tralee more than seventy people picketed the Department of Justice in Dublin in a lunchtime protest. They represented Sinn Fein, the Women's Community Press, the Union of Students of Ireland, the Socialist Workers' Movement and the Dublin Lesbian/Gay Collective. In London twenty women protested outside the Irish Embassy.

On 22 January the Oireachtas Committee on Women's Rights, composed of TDs and senators, called on the Minister for Justice to intervene in the Tribunal. The committee stressed that they did not want to interfere in the judicial system but unanimously agreed to draw the Minister's attention to their concern.

Mary O'Rourke, TD, Fianna Fail spokeswomen on education, said that as a women's rights committee they should speak out. It would be wrong not to bring to the Minister's attention that throughout the country there was widespread disquiet among women and men at the manner and matter, tone and tenor of the cross-examination in some instances.

Fine Gael TD Madeline Taylor-Quinn described the cross-examination as very, very frightening and said the Tribunal appeared to have strayed from its terms of reference. Senator Brian Mullooly of Fianna Fail said that no human being should be subjected to such treatment.

Dr Rory O'Hanlon, TD, Fianna Fail spokesman on health, said

that everybody would like to see more sensitivity in the cross-examination.

Fine Fael TD, Monica Barnes, who chaired the meeting, said they all had feelings of sympathy for the traumatic experience that I and my family were going through. It showed an attitude to women's sexuality that needed to be examined.

Dr Michael Woods, TD, Fianna Fail spokesman on justice, sought to ask the Minister in the Dail if he was aware of widespread public disquiet at what was regarded as the insensitive treatment being given to witnesses. His special notice question was ruled out of order by the Ceann Comhairle.

Fianna Fail TDs Tom McEllistrim and Denis Foley, both from North Kerry, called on the government to confirm that the legal costs of our family would be borne by the state. The Minister said that under legislation passed by the Dail this was a matter solely for the presiding judge.

Charles Haughey, TD, leader of the Fianna Fail party, said people were outraged by the treatment I received at the Tribunal. I had not been arraigned but was there as a witness to help the Tribunal, he said. He condemned the harsh treatment I had received.

The Council for the Status of Women protested to the President of the High Court, Mr Justice Hamilton. "The Council does not understand why any necessary questioning of a witness regarding intimate personal details is not done in camera, as is allowed under the procedural terms of an inquiry such as this."

Nell McCafferty wrote in the *Irish Press:* "We have been given the dates, duration and regularity of Joanne Hayes's menstrual flow in 1981, 1982 and 1983. Also people now know the width of her uterus after her daughter Yvonne was born and even the nature of the material used in her afterbirth stitches. . . . This inquiry is supposed to be about the events in Tralee Garda Station, but so far, due to the nature of the questions asked, it is about mattresses and the men in Joanne Hayes's life and her private behaviour with them."

In the *Irish Independent* Marianne Heron pointed out that if my evidence had been heard in camera so too would the rest of the inquiry. "The application of the law in the Tribunal is little different from the adversary style system used in normal court cases. The practice whereby barristers seek to bully, discredit or even psychologically break witnesses for the other side is a daily routine.

The public are now seeing — in some cases perhaps for the first time — just how cruel and distasteful that system can be, and how ill-suited it is to deal with something like the Joanne Hayes case.

"We have been made fully and graphically aware of the realities of women's biology. No fact of female sexuality has been spared; menstruation, birth, bleeding, lactation, pregnancy . . . The female facts of life have never had such a public airing and many have found its exposure at the Tribunal offensive and have called for private or censored discussion of these subjects."

Poet Brendan Kennelly, in an interview in *Hot Press* magazine, said: "The media coverage and public interest is inexpressibly morbid. It's like some medieval witch-hunt with the victims burning at the stake and the crowd dancing around the fire."

There was a national appeal to "Send a flower to Joanne" and I received bundles of them. The Tralee Women's Action Group began wearing single yellow flowers on their coats as they attended the hearings. From Dublin we heard from a garda with Abbeydorney connections that one of his inspectors was "like a devil" because he had passed a suburban shop offering the flowers for sale to "send to Joanne".

Two telephone callers, both anonymous, were critical of the Abbeydorney people's protest. One lady who claimed to represent 2,500 Dublin housewives phoned one of the organisers and said Jeremiah and I should be thrown into a boghole. The other, who said she was from Abbeydorney parish, blamed me for the fact that Garda Moloney's wife had suffered a miscarriage due to the strain of the case.

In the letters to the papers many speculated about whether the gardai would come under such exposure in the witness box, although the answer was only too obvious.

The Tribunal Continues

JUST WHEN IT seemed that the Tribunal was about to lose its sexual flavour the bizarre details of another case were were introduced. Dr John Fennelly the Limerick psychiatrist was on the stand and Anthony Kennedy reminded him of a case he had worked on in Northern Ireland in which a girl had had delusions about visitations from spirits who had intercourse with her. Dr Brian McCaffrey had worked with Dr Fennelly on that case and the subject had been a dominant personality.

Mr Kennedy wasn't suggesting that I had sexual delusions about spirits. He wanted to know about the domination element because the girl had been able to twist her family to suit her version of the facts and if she changed her mind they changed theirs. Could it apply in this case? Dr Fennelly said he would be very doubtful. I was not dominant and it would be very unusual if they would all admit to a crime that none of them committed no matter how dominant I might be.

Mr Kennedy pointed out that all my family had retracted their confessions. It was my role vis-à-vis theirs that he was interested in.

Dr Fennelly said it was very difficult to see it. He presumed that they had made their confessions separately? Yes, but the retractions may not have been made separately, suggested Mr Kennedy. Dr Fennelly wasn't impressed by the lawyer's speculation.

He told the Tribunal that while he was treating me in Limerick I had told him that I was not the mother of the Caherciveen baby and that the father of my baby was a married man living in Tralee. I said that I had panicked and killed the child by putting my hands on his neck. I had been very depressed, guilty and ashamed of what I had done. I had been very relieved when my baby was found.

He had moved me to hospital because I was possibly suicidal and I had responded very well to anti-depressant drugs. Essentially I had kept to the same account. "The hand around the baby's mouth" was the phrase I had used. I had a guilt feeling about not telling my mother I was pregnant. He said I told him I had intended to keep the baby, and that I had been afraid of Yvonne being taken from me and of going to prison.

Michael Moriarty asked if my account was fully credible.
"We believed her from the start," said Dr Fennelly.

He told Dermot McCarthy that on 2 May I was very distressed and suggestible: I was a very ill girl. He was used to dealing with prisoners and didn't believe everything he was told but after a day he had mentioned to somebody that I was telling the truth.

Martin Kennedy asked Dr Fennelly if I was in love with Jeremiah or with what he or other men did with me. Dermot McCarthy objected to the question and the judge asked what was its relevance. Mr Kennedy said I had had a sexual relationship with a man other than Jeremiah. If he could show to the Tribunal that I was interested in sexual activity for its own sake and not for love of a particular man he would be well down the road to showing that while I was carrying on with Jeremiah I was also carrying on with another man. Carrying on was a euphemism for having sex, Mr Kennedy said.

The judge allowed the question and Dr Fennelly said he believed that I loved Jeremiah. I had also told that to the other doctors. One of my worries had been that he was having a rough time.

Dr Fennelly told Kevin O'Higgins that when he saw me on 2 May I was in a highly suggestible state. On the previous day when I was brought into the garda station the depression could have set in. I would have been exhausted and open to suggestion. It would not have been necessary to use extreme violence to get me to go along with a suggestion. If I had a feeling of guilt about the death of one baby I might easily admit to the death of another. There had been no suggestion to anybody at the hospital that I had had twins.

The judge looked out into the sunshine and announced that it would be a good time to visit the farm. Spring was in the air and it would be bright for another hour or more. He had his outdoor gear in the boot of his car. He always had, he smiled, like an old Boy Scout who had never forgotten the basic rule of Bí Ullamh (Be Prepared). The lawyers who had stood as if to request an adjournment of the safari sat down again without protest. They gathered their papers and made tracks for their cars. The Droumcunnig farm had been tripping off their tongues for six weeks and now on 12 February they would see for themselves. For some, whose contact with the world of agriculture would hardly extend beyond their dining tables, it was a voyage into the unknown.

It was crisp and frosty as the cars pulled up on the roadway outside. We had all been taken unawares by the judge's decision, none more so than the photographers who had their pictures for the day all ready for despatch. Now the media descended in packs, most having cadged lifts in the scatter from the courthouse.

A few locals gathered and watched Judge Lynch in overcoat, hat and wellingtons stride down the path into our yard. Dermot McCarthy borrowed a pair of wellies and somebody else was lucky as well, but the majority of the legal men were in their tribunal footwear. Anthony Kennedy's gleaming black shoes looked to be in danger as he followed the judge towards the muddy gap that led to the fields. Kathleen and I joined them, pointing out when asked the various landmarks that had cropped up in evidence. The tour of duty didn't last long. The area of interest was small and as they returned after completing a half-circle Martin Kennedy caught the whiff from the silage pit. He remarked on it to his namesake but he got no reply. Anthony was holding his breath. The leaders of

Kathleen, Joanne, James Paul MacDonnell, Brian Curtin, Judge Lynch, Dermot McCarthy, Martin Kennedy, Anthony Kennedy, Kevin O'Higgins. (Michael MacSweeney).

the pack halted at what somebody recognised as an electric fence but we assured them that the current had been switched off.

Martin Kennedy had a close look at our front door and thanked somebody for facilitating them and then the rush back to their world started up. Anthony Kenendy's shoes were still gleaming as he walked to his car. There was just one photographer left when somebody though of asking me to cross the ditch near the bedstead as I had done on the night of the birth. I did it twice, as effortlessly as I had claimed in evidence, and then everybody left.

A week later the judge returned, this time accompanied by only a few lawyers, and saw for himself that I had no difficulty with that ditch. As it happened we nearly missed him on his return visit because we were on our way into Tralee to visit Aunt Bridie when we met the cars on the way and we were asked to turn back. That day one of our cows was within hours of having a calf and several times afterwards Kevin O'Higgins enquired about how the calving season was going. Even for us the Tribunal had its moments of humanity.

Given the choice between going to a disco and a hurling match Kathleen would have no problem. She lives for sport. She never misses one of Abbeydorney's matches and even goes in the evenings to watch the teams training. That must rank as the ultimate in enthusiasm because the club has been in the doldrums for quite a few years now but Kate, like Uncle Maurice, loves Abbeydorney.

I felt very guilty now for having got her involved in the mire of the Tribunal. She had never approved of my association with Jeremiah and had asked me to end it.

James Duggan, BL, asked her to recount the events of the night of 12/13 April. She told of noticing that I was sick before she went to get her hair cut and of her concern later when I had gone out the front door as she was getting ready for bed. After a while she had called out to me to ask if I was all right and I had said I'd be in in a minute. When I did come in she had seen drops of blood on the floor and on my nightie.

Next morning after helping Mike with the cows she had gone out the front and seen drops of blood and what she thought was an afterbirth. She had also seen a bag and some gravel and hay and had lifted it with her foot and got afraid and gone home. I had denied to her in February that I was pregnant, but in March when we were in a field cutting briars she could see that I was.

On 13 April she had been concerned about my appearance and had gone that evening to tell Mary Shanahan. Mary had said, "Oh Jesus, she had the baby." She told of accompanying Mary Shanahan and Elsie Moore back to our house and of the conversation we had before going to the doctor.

She had told this to the detective when they called on 1 May. She had taken the detectives to where she had found what she thought was the afterbirth and this had been taken away by Detective McArdle. She had been asked if she minded going to the garda station and she had said she did but she had felt that she had no choice.

When she realised that the detectives were questioning her about the Caherciveen baby she had said, "Oh no, we had nothing to do with it." She had been surprised when the gardai started writing down what she was telling them as it was an indication that they were questioning her on a criminal charge. None of the gardai had ever mentioned anything about twins. All the questioning had been about the Caherciveen baby.

Kathleen told Brendan Grogan that she was suspicious when I went outside the house that I was having a baby and these suspicions were confirmed when I came in and said that I was after having a heavy period. She did not know what I had done with the baby. She thought I had left it outside.

To die? asked Mr Grogan. Kathleen said she did not know, she did not go out that night.

"You were willing to remain silent forever about that?"

"I was waiting for Joanne to tell me. I would have stayed silent forever if she hadn't told me."

The detectives had been very sarcastic and sneering, especially one of them. She had become very frightened of him because he had sat very close to her and was staring at her and breathing very deeply. He was very gruff and said that he had her sister upstairs all day and she was doing nothing but telling lies.

The reason she had denied at first that she knew I was pregnant was that she had thought they would go away if she said she didn't know. She pointed out the incorrect parts of her statement. She said that at one stage she had become very frightened and that was why she had decided to tell the gardai "what they wanted to hear".

She didn't know anybody called Tom Flynn and hadn't written

his name on the mattress.

She said the gardai had got a bit of a shock when they had found my baby on the farm. She and Mike and Ned has searched in the afternoon and Mike had seen the bag and they had told Patrick Mann. He had instructed them to tell the gardai immediately and she had gone to Garda Liam Moloney and reported the find. She had never had any suspicion that the child found in Caherciveen might be mine. "I knew Joanne could never do that to a baby," she said.

Kathleen got a severe grilling in the witness box. Counsel for the gardai put it to her time and again that she had been with me when I gave birth and that she had actually disposed of the body. She cried several times as she denied being involved and kept insisting that we had had nothing to do with the Caherciveen baby. Counsel put it to her that she lost her chance of a proper life because of being used by me to mind Yvonne, but she rejected this proposition as well.

Afterwards she was acknowledged by the press as having been an impressive and convincing witness.

Ned received no such compliments. Many times in response to questions about his statement he said that he had been confused and upset and "up in a heap" when he made it. He had become so totally confused, he said, that at one stage he was convinced that the family had done something wrong and that he had been implicated in the killing of the Caherciveen baby and in disposing of the body at Slea Head. During the twelve hours of interrogation in Tralee station he had become so fearful and upset that he had concocted a false account of what happened, he testified.

He told Dermot McCarthy that he had been disappointed about my continuing association with Jeremiah Locke. He had suspected in February that I was expecting but he had not said anything. He had not wished to face the problem. It had come as a shock to him in Tralee garda station on 1 May when Detective Sergeant Dillon and Detective Garda Mahoney told him they were investigating the death of the Caherciveen baby.

Anthony Kennedy said at one stage that Ned has answered "I don't know" to about fifty questions and on another occasion told him to "stop acting the gom".

Ned said he would have worried about a "mi-adh" (curse) on the family if a baby were to be buried on the land. If he had wanted to dispose of a baby in the sea Banna and Ballyheigue and Ballybunion would have been closer than Slea Head.

Ned said afterwards that his mind had gone blank in the witness box. Not alone had he become almost inarticulate but he had been unable to think properly. He knew that he had not done himself justice. Friends who were present during his evidence said he had dripped with perspiration at times and had appeared to be extremely nervous. This was unusual for him as he is normally sociable and relaxed and has taken part in a stage production of the play *Da* by the local dramatic society. One can only assume that the ordeal of giving evidence to the Tribunal after all the pressure of the previous months had been too much for him.

On Wednesday 30 January the Tribunal was transferred to Tralee General Hospital to hear the evidence of my Aunt Bridie Fuller. She had been admitted to the hospital two days earlier. However, Dr Robert McEneaney, consultant physician at the hospital, said he did not think that Bridie was capable of giving evidence or of being examined or cross-examined. She had suffered a certain degree of brain damage from a stroke and this had resulted in her being somewhat disoriented, and slurred in her speech. Her intellectual faculties were quite good, he said, but she had difficulty in expressing her thoughts and ideas. At present she was unable to understand legal advice or to instruct her lawyers. He said it was reasonable to assume that she would make a recovery to the point where she could give evidence to the Tribunal, possibly in two weeks.

Mike is the farmer in our family, hardworking and uncomplicated. Among our friends he is everybody's favourite. Even the gardai were not surprised that he hadn't noticed that I was pregnant. They and Dr Fennelly and even Mom had described him as not being very intelligent, although the gardai had added that he possessed "a high degree of native cunning". He spends very little time in the house, dashes in for his meals and gets back to his work as quickly as possible. His life revolves around the farm and his daily visits to neighbours and to the village and he has no time for television or other distractions such as sport. The Tribunal was a nuisance because it interrupted his routine but the gravity of the issues never got through to him.

His evidence was predictably confusing, both for him and for the lawyers. On the night of his first day's testimony he went to the Silver Dollar pub in Abbeydorney as he did most nights. Sometimes he would have a pint of beer and on other occasions he had a rock shandy, a mixture of lemonade and orange squash.

In the lounge Jerome O'Donovan and John Barrett were having a drink with three journalists: Mary Cummins of *The Irish Times*, Nell McCafferty of the *Irish Press* and Anne Cadwallader, Dublin correspondent of the BBC. Mike sat in a corner on his own and bought his own drink but shortly afterwards one of the journalists ordered a drink for him when buying a round for the others and they asked him if the calves that he had been worrying about had arrived yet. Even the lawyers knew that Mike was more concerned about the calving season than the Tribunal.

Next morning when Mike resumed his evidence a note was passed to Anthony Kennedy and Mike was asked if he had been involved in a conference with some press people in an Abbeydorney pub the night before. Mike tried to explain what had occurred but he didn't even know who the journalists were. It wasn't a critical issue in the Tribunal but it was disconcerting to find that there was a "mole" in our little village, and the journalists were extremely annoyed.

Mike's cross-examination was drawing to an end when James Duggan asked him where had the baby been born. "In the room above mine" Mike replied. Who was present? Mike didn't know, he hadn't been there anyway, he said. Had Bridie been present? No, I had given birth on my own.

We were upset when we heard the news but we didn't blame Mike. He said he had got mixed up and had been getting ready to step down when the question had come. He had heard one of us saying that the gardai were alleging that the baby had been born in my bedroom and he had thought that the question referred to the allegation. As far as he was concerned there would have been no point in asking him about the actual birth because he knew nothing about it. He had other things on his mind.

It has been suggested that it was only after Mr Duggan had explained to Mike the meaning of an oath that he said that the baby was born in the house, the inference being that Mr Duggan's explanation had frightened him into an admission. In fact, Mr Duggan had asked at least ten questions between explaining about the oath and asking where the baby was born and in that interval Mike would have long forgotten the impact of what Mr Duggan had been trying to get across to him. It is most unfair to suggest otherwise and a gross exaggeration of Mike's ability to absorb such information.

Next day, Wednesday 6 January, the Tribunal returned to Tralee General Hospital. Aunt Bridie was brought in a wheelchair to assist the Tribunal and a nurse and the matron stood behind her as the photographers went into action. The judge had instructed the lawyers to adopt an informal pose when speaking to her. In fact people who were present say she was treated like a child. The problem as far as we were concerned was whether the judge might have taken her evidence seriously.

Auntie Bridie had been in poor health for some years. Even before she retired prematurely in 1978 she had been deteriorating and had become careless about her appearance. She began to drink heavily, wine or sherry mostly, and this was a big worry to us. She would get up at around 1.00 in the morning and would drink wine if she had it. Usually she went to bed for a few hours in the afternoon and always retired for the night at 7.00, only to reappear again in the early hours of the morning. She had stopped driving the car at the request of Auntie Aquinas who had heard about her drinking habits.

She had also stopped drinking after a year or so but maintained her irregular routine within the house and continued to deteriorate. Gone was the brisk erect gait that people had always admired. She suffered a stroke early in 1984 and was in hospital in Cork, Tralee and Killarney at various times. To us she appeared to be growing increasingly senile.

On 3 January when her own doctor was no longer in Tralee Kathleen and I called to Doctor Ray Chute in Tralee and told him that she was not taking her tablets and that we were worried about whether or not she was capable of giving evidence to the Tribunal. We asked him to call to see her as he had known her as a nurse. Dr Chute had called the following day and decided that she was fit to give evidence. We had accepted his decision although we did not agree that he was right. She had become difficult even in such matters as refusing to take her tablets and seemed to take pleasure in defying everybody's wishes. We didn't know what she was going to say in evidence because we had never discussed it with her, but we knew she was liable to say anything. I don't deny that we were worried.

In evidence Aunt Bridie said that on the night or early morning of 7 April I had delivered the baby myself in my bedroom and she had assisted. She had cut the umbilical cord because the baby was chesty; she needed a suction pump but did not have one. She did not break the waters — that stage had passed — and she never thought of getting medical help. The baby had cried but she had not been present when he died.

Michael Moriarty pointed out that the date of 7 April differed from the date mentioned in other evidence but suggested that perhaps she was not too definite about it. She replied that it was the right date.

The judge decided that Auntie Bridie should not be subjected to too much questioning that day and said they would resume at the hospital two days later.

That afternoon the Tribunal switched back to the courthouse and my Aunt Joan told the judge that in her opinion Aunt Bridie, whom she had last met at Christmas, had grown feeble-minded and was not responsible for what she was saying. She did not think Aunt Bridie was fit to give evidence. She also said that she had not objected to my being pregnant but she did not like the idea of breaking up a marriage.

Aunt Joan, who has been slightly deaf for some time and speaks with a strong, assertive voice, which apparently grated on some of the Tribunal personnel, said she was very fond of Yvonne and was on very good terms with me although I had resented her suggestion that Yvonne should be adopted when I had been pregnant with her.

Next day Dr Chute told the Tribunal that when Kathleen and

I had called to him we had asked him to issue a certificate that Aunt Bridie was incapable of giving evidence. He had known her as a ward nurse for over twenty years and she had been a first class nurse. When he called to see her he found her general condition to be quite good and she was not in any way mentally deficient. He had rung Patrick Mann to tell him that he was unable to issue the certificate.

Dr McEneaney was recalled to give evidence about Aunt Bridie's condition. He said he had examined her on five occasions since he had told the Tribunal the previous week that she was temporarily unfit to give evidence. She had improved faster than might have been expected, he said. Her mental capacity was quite good and her orientation, powers of recall and concentration were good too. He said that he had made his decision two days previously and he believed that she was a fully competent witness.

Now it was my mother's turn, poor Mom who had already become bewildered by the sequence of events, the daily ordeal at the Tribunal and the endless speculation among our friends. She preferred to attend, even when she was not allowed into the courtroom while the family were giving evidence, because she said she would be worrying on her own at home. So she worried at the courthouse, tried to keep up with the chatter and after each hearing would ask some reliable observer how things had gone that day.

For some years she had suffered from blood pressure and a chest problem that severely curtailed her activity. She didn't go anywhere any more, she was brought, and her decision-making was restricted to what she would choose from the shelves of the local supermarket. She went to mass every week and visited the church whenever the opportunity arose and if we went to evening mass we would take her for a drink afterwards. Basically, however, her life was confined to the kitchen of our home.

She suffered in the witness box for being a devout Catholic. She said that the statements she had made to the detectives who had questioned her contained many details which were untrue and which had been put in on the insistence of the two detectives. They had suggested things to her and had refused to accept her denials. She denied that I had had the baby in my bedroom and had stabbed the baby and that it had been taken away and thrown into the sea.

Anthony Kennedy put it to her that she seemed anxious to

establish that she was a religious and pious woman and Mom said she expected that she was. Should she commit perjury and die on the spot, did she believe she would be condemned for all eternity? She did. Did she believe that as part of her religion? She did. Was she still sticking to her story? She was because she was telling the truth. "God, glory be to him, knows that," she said.

I had been only about fifteen, she said, when Dad died and I had been brought up by herself and Aunt Bridie. She had not approved of my association with Jeremiah and had been very shocked when she heard I was expecting Yvonne. She had told me I should not have anything to do with Jeremiah but I was over twenty-one and it was a matter for myself. She was very fond of Yvonne and she helped Kathleen to look after her while I was at work, she said.

Mr Kennedy asked her if she was surprised at the evidence Dr Chute had given. "I suppose I was, I don't know," she replied. He asked her if she knew what nobbling a witness meant and explained that it meant either getting a witness not to give evidence or to change the evidence. Mom said we were not trying to do anything. Had we tried to get Aunt Bridie to go to Mr Mann and row in with the rest of us? It was up to her to give her own statement. Was it not obvious that if she did not renounce her statement there would be total conflict between her statement and what we told Mr Mann? Were we not worried about trying to bring Aunt Bridie around to our way of thinking? Yes, we were worried all right, Mom said.

Anthony Kennedy asked if Mom knew about the attempt by her two daughters to have Bridie certified as incapable. Mom said it was not an attempt. We had gone in to see Dr Chute and he had come out to the house to see Bridie. Were we upset that he would not play ball? It was up to Dr Chute to give the certificate or not.

Mr Kennedy reminded Mom of an occasion when Garda Moloney had met her coming from confession. He had asked her if she had confessed what was in her statement. She told the Tribunal that she had to confess all her sins. Mr Kennedy said Garda Moloney had been referring to her confession on 29 April before she had been interviewed by the gardai. What had she been confessing then? he asked.

"It is only to the priest I tell my sins," Mom replied.

"And certainly not to me," Anthony Kennedy smiled.

Michael Moriarty asked her if she thought Aunt Bridie was a

reliable witness. Mom said she was not a doctor, but she did not think she was capable of giving good evidence.

Aunt Bridie completed her evidence on Friday 8 February. Dermot McCarthy who was inhibited insofar as she was his client, put it to her that Dr Harbison had said he could not state that the baby had lived, that its lungs had not been inflated and that her evidence seemed to indicate that the child had lived. Aunt Bridie said that was correct. She said she was quite sure that Ned and Mike had not driven the car anywhere that night. She agreed that at Tralee garda station she had not made any admission about my pregnancy or the birth of the baby until she and I had met and talked.

Asked if the baby had been washed she said it had not been washed because it had been a bit chesty. She had been afraid that if she washed it she might upset it and it was not strong enough to be washed. After 13 April the baby's body was no longer to be found and nobody had told her where it was and she had not asked anybody. She had asked me where the body of the child was and I had not told her. Had I told her I had hidden it on the land? Yes.

Anthony Kennedy began by telling her about the compliments Dr Chute had paid her the previous day. She agreed that there had been "a fair bit of panic" in the house on the night of the birth and that I had been hysterical and that she was doing the best she could during the long night.

She was concerned that they should get antiseptic and she had got Dettol and Kathleen had got warm water. She had washed the baby thoroughly, she told Mr Kennedy.

Michael Moriarty asked her if she remembered breaking the waters. She said she had done that. Mr Moriarty reminded her that two days earlier she had said she might not have broken the waters. Now she replied that she remembered that she did help to break the waters.

Martin Kennedy asked about Tom Flynn. She remembered buying the mattress, but the name Tom Flynn was not on it when she bought it.

She told Kevin O'Higgins that all the members of our family had seen the baby at some stage that night and that the baby had lived for some hours. There had been no mention of twins in the house that night, she said.

The judge smiled at Aunt Bridie and thanked her and said that she had been a great help.

Sister Aquinas was the last member of our family to give evidence. Accompanied by two nuns from her convent in Ballybunion she had to face a merciless intrusion from the cameramen outside the courthouse. It was bad enough for her at the age of seventy-three to be linked with such a sordid event through family circumstances without having to be exposed to the world on film as well.

She told the Tribunal that my relationship with Jeremiah had caused her sadness and that she had written to me pointing out the seriousness of a relationship with a married man and the breaking up of a family. She recalled that she had offered to help me about Yvonne's birth and getting her adopted if I wished. When she had visited our home on St Patrick's Day, 17 March 1984, she had noticed that my face was pale and thin. She had thought that I was feeling the effects of having had Yvonne. She had no idea that I was pregnant.

Anthony Kennedy, whom she had taught at Moyderwell Convent in Tralee during his first years at school, asked her if she was not remarkably unobservant not to have noticed that I was pregnant five weeks prior to the birth of my last child. She said she was not unobservant. He was not suggesting that she was lying but hadn't she noticed that I was pregnant with Yvonne three months before the birth? She had. How did she explain it then? She couldn't explain it.

Mr Kennedy asked about a visit she had made to our home in late May or early June. She remembered it all right, she said, because Bridie was upset and she had asked Bridie was she involved. No, Bridie had said, but she had changed her statement to the gardai because she thought it would help me. (Prior to making her statement late on 1 May, Bridie had denied even knowing that I had been pregnant.)

The judge asked Auntie Aquinas why it mattered so much to our family whether he believed that the baby had been born in the field rather than in the house. Poor Aquinas tried to convey to the judge that it was important for us to be believed because it was the truth. Was Bridie lying then? Not necessarily: to Bridie a changed statement would not constitute a lie in Bridie's mental condition.

She said I was the dominant member of our family, which came as a surprise to me.

Judge Lynch referred more than once to our insistence on being believed about the birth in the field. He called it an obsession at one stage and didn't seem to understand that to us it was all-important that our story should be believed because it was the truth. At the Tribunal we weren't on trial regarding the birth but our veracity and our honour were at stake and that, however insignificant it may have been in the legal technicalities of reaching a conclusion, meant everything to us.

Since speculation became virtually the order of the day at various stages of the Tribunal it may be worth offering a theory of a couple of Aunt Bridie's former nursing colleagues about her evidence. Both women nursed with her for many years and had been close personal friends of hers for more than thirty years. They believe that Bridie, unwilling to admit even to herself that I could have been pregnant and given birth in a field without her knowledge, and not realising the gravity of the situation due to her increasing senility, simply created a scenario in which she did everything according to the rules or as well as she could have done in the circumstances in any case. They believe that she was speaking not from reality but from basic professional pride.

A few weeks after Aunt Bridie had completed her evidence one of her former colleagues was entering the Tribunal when she met a Tralee garda who was involved in the case. "How is Bridie, have you seen her lately?" he asked. She said she had been to see her that day.

"And how is she?" he asked.

"I'm afraid I can't give you the answer you'd like to hear," she said. "Bridie is away in the clouds."

An expert in oceanography, Professor Brian Barry of University College Galway, told the Tribunal that it was a remote possibility that an object such as an infant child thrown into the sea at Slea Head on the night of 12 April would later have been washed up on White Strand, Caherciveen. It was much more likely that the

Cahirciveen baby came from a southern direction and he accepted that the baby could have been dumped from a passing ship.

Replying to Anthony Kennedy, Professor Barry agreed that local fishermen would have much more information. To counter Professor Barry's evidence the gardai called a Dingle fisherman and boat builder Nicholas "Sugar" O'Connor, but Mr O'Connor agreed with almost everything that Professor Barry had said.

It was Thursday 21 February and the Tribunal was tidying up loose ends before moving to Dublin Castle. Joseph Kelliher, manager of the furniture department at McElligotts in Castleisland, took the stand. Immaculately dressed in a tweed suit Mr Kelliher hardly seemed aware of the importance of the knowledge he was about to share with the rest of the country. In the witness box he was relaxed and chatty but a stickler for detail.

The mattress was unrolled on the courtroom floor beside him. It was a three-inch-thick foam mattress and I noticed a few tears on the green-brown cover that had not been on it before it left our house. Mr Kelliher recognised it as one that he could have sold but didn't recall selling it to Aunt Bridie.

Did he know Tom Flynn, Mr Duggan asked. He did.

Judge Lynch sat forward on his seat, hands clasped under his chin, elbows firmly on the bench.

All Ireland is agog to know about him at this stage; who is he? Mr Duggan inquired, visibly struggling to stay serious.

Mr Kelliher said a young fellow called Tom Flynn had worked in McElligotts' furniture department from September 1968 to the summer of 1969 and had gone to England. His mother had told Mr Kelliher that Tom had gone to America from there and had got married and had never returned.

Would Mr Kelliher know Tom's signature? No.

Martin Kennedy who had introduced Tom Flynn to the cast in hushed drama on 8 January added a touch of comedy for his exit. He told Judge Lynch that he would like to examine the mattress before questioning the witness.

"It's there," the judge smiled, gesturing with the palm of his hand to where red-faced gardai stood holding it.

The lawyer walked within inches of us, head down, gamely retaining his stern expression while the public giggled expectantly. What was he going to do or find? He fingered the mattress gingerly in the manner of a man who had suddenly discovered how some of the other half live, then inspected the signature which one of the gardai showed him. He nodded his thanks to the gardai and strode back to his place while the mattress was folded again.

He had a few questions for Mr Kelliher. Weren't all mattresses wrapped in plastic when sold? Yes, but not all. Were staff in the habit of autographing furniture before it left the shop? No. Flynn and Tom were both common names? Yes. It could be anyone? Yes. It could be by a girl to remind her of her boyfriend? Yes, it could have been written before the mattress left the factory. Wasn't it unlikely that anyone from the factory would do this? It was possible.

Anything is possible, Mr Kennedy said, resigned apparently to the fact that his long shot had come unstuck. Tom Flynn was alive and well and a long way from Castleisland. We heard no more of him.

Wish me luck, Patrick Mann whispered as we went into the courtroom on the afternoon of Thursday 21 February. Tom Flynn had been laughed out of court and our lunch had gone down well but now Patrick had to take the hot seat and you could cut the buzz with a knife.

In direct evidence he recalled being told by Ban Gharda O'Regan on the morning of 2 May at Tralee District Court that somebody wanted to see him in the consultation room. He had found me crying and distressed and I had shown him a photocopy of the charge sheet. I had told him, "They are trying to say that I killed the baby in Caherciveen, Patrick." After being remanded in custody I had spoken to him again for a few minutes and Kathleen had come in and asked me where I had put the baby and had explained that her head was so muddled that she couldn't remember what I had told her the previous night.

He said that he had found Aunt Bridie vague on the occasions that he had met her. If she had gone to him in May 1984 and asked him to draw up her will he would have had doubts about doing it. He had also found it very difficult to take instructions from Mike.

Patrick's rapid-fire delivery was a problem for the stenographers and occasionally he was asked to slow down. Anthony Kennedy, deliberate and polished, set the stage for some bitter counterpunching. "Isn't that incredible?" he seethed when Patrick said he had not kept notes of consultations with us. Patrick explained that he had been waiting for the book of evidence to be served before taking instructions about our defence. He had opened his files for inspection and had been forthright with the Tribunal at all times. He resented the suggestion that he would hold anything back.

Wasn't I very composed after the District Court remand compared with how I had been beforehand? "Not very composed. She was more composed than she had been earlier but she wasn't as composed as you and I are now, Mr Kennedy."

Anthony Kennedy suggested that it was remarkable that Patrick had not "exploded" on hearing about my baby being found on the farm. Patrick said he found out that a baby and a bag had been found on the farm and at that stage he knew he had the ideal defence to the murder charge.

Mr Kennedy referred to what he regarded as an unnecessary delay in bringing my bail application before the High Court. It was common for judges to be called from their beds in the middle of the night to deal with such applications, he said. Patrick said he understood that such applications of bail were made on Fridays in the High Court and Dermot McCarthy asked the judge, "I wonder does my friend (Anthony Kennedy) know the difference between a habeas corpus and a bail application?" The judge indicated that Patrick was right and we nudged each other in delight.

When the judge rose just before one o'clock on Friday 22 February Tralee had seen the last of the Tribunal. Locals felt cheated because they were being denied the opportunity of seeing most of the garda witnesses. One man had taken a week's holiday just to attend and now for him it was over at half-time.

Contrary to what one reporter wrote we were dreading the switch to Dublin. We would be leaving our supporters and we did not know what to expect in our new surroundings. There were fears that we might encounter some antagonism but these proved unfounded. We had got permission to bring Yvonne and a neighbour to mind her but at the last minute we decided to leave her at home for the first week while we decided whether it would be suitable for her. Our neighbour and friend Helen O'Donovan and her husband John offered to look after her for us and when we found that the Dublin set-up would have been very inconvenient for her the O'Donovans insisted on keeping her with them right to the end of the Tribunal. We used to collect her on Friday nights when we arrived from Dublin and returned her to Helen and John on Sunday evenings prior to leaving for Dublin. I can never thank them enough for what they did for us. Another neighbour Sheila Fitzmaurice also helped to look after Yvonne during my absence, especially by taking her to Tralee for a treat a couple of times each week.

Kathleen and I shared a twin-bedded room at the Ormond Hotel on Ormond Quay, just a five-minute walk from Dublin Castle. This was paid for by the state and we were allowed breakfast, lunch and an evening meal (not to cost more than £6). When Ned and Mike travelled to hear the evidence of the gardai who had interrogated them they too were allowed their hotel and train expenses. We became very friendly with some of the hotel staff, especially Maureen, Jane, and the two Harrys and were helped to feel at home although they seemed to be at pains to avoid mentioning the Tribunal at any time.

Arrangements were made to enable us to collect our welfare money at the Labour Exchange in Townsend Street each Thursday morning and several Kerry people who were in Dublin on business called to the hotel to wish us well. Yet we missed home a lot and phoned Helen O'Donovan a couple of times each day to inquire about Yvonne. She used to recognise my voice on the phone and would call my name but she didn't miss me too much because she had Helen's two little boys to play with.

Dublin Castle, for all its magnificence in size and design, is grey and impersonal and surrounds a huge yard that instantly reminded me of the exercise area in Limerick Jail. The Tribunal was conducted in a conference hall which adjoined the Great Hall of the Castle. It was an appropriate setting for what many saw as the annihilation of an Irish family, because in centuries past it had been the seat of the ruling British Ascendancy. James Connolly had spent his last days there and many republicans had been executed within its walls. Nowadays many civil service departments are based there and countless foreign dignitaries, including Margaret Thatcher, have stayed in the state apartments while on offical visits.

Patrick Mann had the distinction of being the link between the two venues but Anthony Kennedy could not complete his cross-examination due to suffering conjunctivitis and his namesake Martin took over. We took our places in the front row of the section reserved for witnesses and between us sat Patrick's sister, Annette O'Connor, who had left her boutique in Abbeyfeale to lend some family support.

Patrick agreed that he had taken no instructions from us up to 10 October. Why hadn't I made any allegations against the Gardai until after the charges were dropped? Kennedy asked. Patrick said that it had not been necessary. If somebody complained of a broken arm or anything like that he would complain right away but the allegations were not of that nature and he was reserving them as part of my defence.

He said that I had made no allegations against the gardai on 2 May but that on 5 May at the hospital in Limerick I had given him on account of what had happened at the garda station. Patrick said he had advised us that we could take a civil action about our allegations or we could use them for our defence and that had been the course he had recommended.

He said we had told him that we thought that Aunt Bridie might not be capable of giving evidence and he had told us that a doctor would have to give evidence to the Tribunal to that effect. We had agreed to go to Dr Hayes, Aunt Bridie's doctor, but had discovered that he had taken up a position in Cork. Patrick Reidy had then mentioned Dr Chute and Dr Chute had subsequently rung back to say that he had been to see her and in his opinion Aunt Bridie was fit to give evidence, but he felt that she should be examined by the family doctor. Martin Kennedy said his interpretation was that we had asked him to certify her as being incapable of giving evidence. Patrick said that was not his interpretation.

Regarding the garda inquiry, Patrick said he had been instructed by us that we did not wish to take part in a question and answer session. He had told the superintendents this and had offered to supply statements from us in reply to any questions they might wish to put. He said he had discussed the question of immunity for me with the superintendents as I could still have been charged with concealment.

Patrick ended his evidence on the afternoon of 27 February after an absorbing battle of wits that had lasted three days.

An Immovable Force

THE GARDAI HAD to be admired for their unrelenting faith and flawless harmony. Without exception they believed our confessions of 1 May and explained that the contradictions contained in them actually proved their veracity. Statements, they said, never matched up in perfect detail anyway. The harmony was incredibly consistent as, one after the other, they related almost word for word that Superintendent Courtney had indicated that we were to be treated with kindness and courtesy; we were free to leave Tralee garda station at any time prior to making our statements, which had been given freely and voluntarily without any garda pressure; and the discovery of my baby at Abbeydorney had simply been a development. The forensic findings proved that I had given birth to twins. No assault, however minor, had occurred in the taking of any statement.

The performance had an early hiccup when Sergeant Patrick Reidy of Caherciveen revealed that the bags found near the body of the Caherciveen baby had not been tested for fingerprints and, worse still, they had vanished from Tralee garda station and were still missing.

Superintendent John Sullivan and Superintendent Donal O'Sullivan outlined their roles in the investigation and detailed conferences and meetings that had taken place. When Superintendent O'Sullivan mentioned that they had discussed the difference in blood groups and also the possibility of another baby in Dingle Bay, Judge Lynch intervened to ask where did that leave him. He interpreted the evidence of Superintendent O'Sullivan to mean that I had had twins but that the Caherciveen baby was not one of them. Now there was a third baby involved. Our family had been cross-examined on the basis that there were twins and that the Caherciveen baby was one of those twins. It had not been put to us that there might be another baby involved. The blood discrepancy had been explained as firstly being caused by contamination of the sample, giving an A reading for what was really an O; secondly, that it might be a weak O masked by an A; and thirdly that it might be an A but that I was having intercourse with somebody else other than Jeremiah Locke at the time. "I have to sort all this out at some stage and where am I left now?" the judge asked.

When Dermot McCarthy rose to cross-examine Superintendent O'Sullivan he was on trial in a way. Members of the public had wondered whether he would be firm enough to deal with the senior garda witnesses. He soon showed that he too could dig deep although he never resorted to the kind of probing of personal life that had been a feature of our treatment in the box. He began by paying a compliment to Superintendent O'Sullivan. Patrick Mann had told him that the superintendent was a very conscientious officer. Then he asked him if he had worked on many cases with Detective Superintendent Courtney. He said he had worked on two kidnapping cases with the detective superintendent.

Hadn't there been a consistent pattern of controversial confessions during Detective Courtney's time in the Technical Branch? There had been controversy all right but Superintendent O'Sullivan wasn't aware of the extent of it. He didn't know if Detective Courtney's unit had a nickname but it had been called the Heavy Gang in the seventies. He did not think the term had come from within the gardai but, yes, he had heard that it had come from the gardai to the newspapers.

Dermot McCarthy asked who had invented the Twins Theory and the superintendent said he resented the word "invented". The theory had arisen because of my two conflicting statements. He agreed that it would be extremely difficult to establish that I was the mother of the Caherciveen baby. Would he accept that the converse probability that I was not the mother of the Caherciveen baby was more likely? Possibility, he said. He agreed that despite that the report had recommended that charges be laid in respect of the Caherciveen baby.

Dermot McCarthy said the third baby that had been mentioned had become jokingly known as the Azores baby among the legal teams. Were there two babies floating around Dingle Bay in plastic bags on the same night? It was a possibility.

Dermot McCarthy suggested that every possibility had been considered except that the statements were untrue. Superintendent O'Sullivan said they were satisfied that the statements were true because of the manner in which they were taken and also because the members who had taken them were responsible gardai.

Dermot McCarthy suggested that the statements had been

written, produced and directed by Detective Superintendent Courtney and the superintendent said he would absolutely deny that. Dermot McCarthy pointed to discrepancies in the statements in which Ned and Mike said they had travelled together to Slea Head. Mike had said they had put a big stone into the bag containing the baby and that Ned had put the bag in the boot of the car. Ned had said that he put the bag on the floor of the car behind the driver's seat and Kathleen in her statement had put herself into the car, whereas in Ned and Mike's statements she had been left behind.

Superintendent O'Sullivan agreed that it could not be true as stated in Kathleen's statement that a person standing on the road to Slea Head could have seen a bag containing a body floating in the sea. Wasn't this one very important portion of the statements that wasn't true? There were discrepancies, Superintendent O'Sullivan said.

Asked how well he knew his detectives in Tralee, Superintendent O'Sullivan said he knew them exceptionally well. They were all men he could rely on absolutely. How many of them had recently been convicted of assault? Two were recently convicted on charges of assault. Had the allegations been made by the person being questioned? Yes.

Who were they? Detective Sergeant Tim O'Callaghan and Detective Garda Con O'Sullivan. Their appeals were entered for the next sitting of the Circuit Court, having been postponed due to the Tribunal. (The convictions were subsequently quashed by the Circuit Court.)

Superintendent O'Sullivan agreed that it was extraordinary that the bags found in Caherciveen had disappeared. He accepted that there were discrepancies in the bags shown to our family. There was a fertiliser bag and a turf bag and all the bags were put to our family and whatever bag was offered to us we accepted. He agreed that Dr Harbison had said that our carving knife was unlikely to have been the murder weapon but he had not ruled it out completely.

Dermot McCarthy said the superintendent was relying on the confessions to the exclusion of forensic science, medical science, the weather, the tides and the wind. Superintendent O'Sullivan said he was relying on the statements because they were taken in a proper manner. Was the Caherciveen baby a twin of my baby? The Superintendent said he had a doubt. A reasonable doubt? A doubt. Didn't he know that in prosecuting a case a conviction could only be obtained by being able to prove against all reasonable doubt? Yes.

Kevin O'Higgins, referring to the Twins Theory, suggested that if I had carried twins weighing five pounds and six pounds plus the other weight factors involved I would have looked enormous and the superintendent said he accepted that. He also agreed that no information had come to hand that I had had a boyfriend other than Jeremiah Locke.

Superintendent O'Sullivan told Judge Lynch that if my baby had been found between 4 and 5 p.m. on 1 May, I and my family would have been eliminated from the investigation into the Caherciveen baby and he would have sent word to Superintendent Sullivan in Caherciveen to reactivate the investigation.

Ban Gharda Nora Maher told Brian Curtin that in her six years in the force she could not recall having previously been asked to record in the station diary the names of people who were in the station helping the gardai with their enquiries.

Garda Finbarr O'Connor, who had been station orderly in Tralee garda station from 10 o'clock in the morning until 2 o'clock in the afternoon, said that between 12.30 and 1 o'clock he had been requested to make entries in the station diary. Who had requested him? To the best of his belief it was Superintendent O'Sullivan. Whose names had he entered? Joanne Hayes, Jeremiah Locke, Ned Hayes, Michael Hayes and Bridie Fuller.

Garda Liam Moloney saw his role in Abbeydorney as a combination of policeman, social worker, marriage counsellor and community stalwart, a Jim'll-fix-it in uniform. He said he knew our family quite well. There had been shock in the community towards the end of 1983 when rumours began circulating about my pregnancy. He recalled questioning me at Tralee garda station on 1 May and recalled my denials and various accounts of my recent pregnancy prior to my confessing to having had a baby on the farm. He denied mentioning the Caherciveen baby or blood groupings to me and that Detective Superintendent Courtney had prodded me with his finger. He also denied receiving a map or sketch from me. He didn't believe my story because I had given him four different versions altogether. He had been present when Kathleen gave her statement that I had stabbed and strangled the baby and he believed her statement. He was aware that in major murder investigations, such as the Yorkshire Ripper case, the police often get spontaneous unguided confessions that turn out to be untrue.

Dermot McCarthy asked if Garda Moloney was joining some of his superior officers in the mental gymnastics that had taken place since the discovery of my baby. He said he believed our statements to be true. We had all signed them. He said that on the day my baby was discovered he had said to a colleague, "If there is another baby here she had twins."

Dermot McCarthy pointed to misspellings of the words "umbilical", "choked" and "boot" in both his notes and Kathleen's statement and suggested that he had prepared his notes on his interview with Kathleen after he had seen her typed statement. Garda Moloney said he had no explanation for the common misspellings other than that it was a coincidence.

He said that since the case began there had been abusive and threatening phone calls to his family and friends and his wife had been very upset and had suffered a miscarriage. When he had completed his evidence Dermot McCarthy said that my family wished to state that they had no connection whatever with any threatening or abusive calls. (On 25 April Garda Moloney left Abbeydorney on a requested transfer to Cork city. He said he would have liked to stay on in Abbeydorney but his wife did not wish to do so.)

Ban Gharda Ursula O'Regan said she saw me laugh and smile while I was interviewed by herself and Detective Garda Stephen Brew and it surprised her. She told the Tribunal that it also surprised her that I could be so happy and so calm and relaxed telling something like that. I was very cool and calm too in the taxi on the way to Limerick jail. Brian Curtin asked her if she was aware that Dr Fennelly, who is a trained psychiatrist, had described me as a very ill girl with suicidal tendencies on the same day that Ban Gharda O'Regan was talking about. She was. Was she saying that her description of my being cool and calm and casual was compatible with Dr Fennelly's evidence? Her evidence was her opinion of me that day, she said. Had she any psychiatric training? No.

The gloom of Dublin Castle seemed to emanate from the witness box. Listening to the garda evidence became almost intolerable as successive witnesses reeled off the same story of kindness and courtesy that was extended to us and our calm and relaxed demeanour under interrogation. There was an answer for everything and a blanket denial of any charge of impropriety.

On instructions from our legal advisers either Kathleen or I stayed in the Tribunal at all times. We were to make notes and pass on questions or clarify issues for the lawyers, but it quickly became a tedious exercise in the face of the garda evidence. More and more I elected to remain outside, either in our room or in the cafeteria, and one day both Kathleen and I were out at the same time. I was in our room reading a transcript and Kathleen was in the cafeteria when Patrick Mann's secretary Helen Brosnan came rounding us up.

Apparently Judge Lynch had noticed that we were both missing and he had halted proceedings while Helen went looking for us. He rebuked us and said that it was in our own interests to be present throughout the sittings. The claustrophobic effect became worse then and I began to hate the building with its long passages where we were constantly coming face to face with the gardai and the opposition lawyers. Towards the end most of the lawyers used to salute us, and a few of the gardai did as well, but Martin Kennedy continued to ignore us.

One morning as we went across the yard we noticed that a window in Martin Kennedy's new Mercedes was down and Kathleen told Brian Curtin about it. At the time the joyriding was at its peak in Dublin. Brian passed on the message to Martin Kennedy who thanked him and said that the window was in fact broken but that the thought was appreciated all the same.

The judge didn't appreciate Brian Curtin's attempt to raise the question of a conviction for assault against Detective Sergeant Tim O'Callaghan. Judge Lynch asked what the purpose was in raising the matter. He was trying the case, he said. He asked Brian Curtin why he was complicating matters by introducing things which had nothing to do with the case. Brian Curtin replied that he would be failing in his duty to us if he did not do so. I had no allegations to make against Detective Sergeant O'Callaghan but I felt that the question was more relevant than some of the questions that had been asked of Jeremiah and myself.

Detective Sergeant Mossie O'Donnell said that Kathleen's allegations that he had made insulting remarks to her and about our family were scurrilous and false and had upset him even to that day. He said he and Detective Sergeant Tim O'Callaghan had interviewed Kathleen for two and three-quarter hours and they had stressed to her that they were not saying that the Caherciveen baby was mine but that it was important that my baby was found. Kathleen had described events taking place at our house but she would never agree that I had given birth to a baby. He had found that strange. He was very surprised to hear a short time later that she was making a statement.

He described removing the bag from a pool on our farm and said Kathleen moved back when he said there was a child in it.

He said he recalled specifically that Dr Harbison said, "Gentlemen, we have a separate existence," at the post mortem next day.

He had contacted a psychiatrist friend, Dr Brendan Lynch of Killarney, who explained the syndromes involved in infanticide. These were: mercy killings, battered babies, the elimination of nuisance and the Medea syndrome, which involved the mother destroying the child to get at the father. Dr Lynch believed that because of the injuries the killing of the Caherciveen baby involved panic and frenzy.

Detective Sergeant O'Donnell, based in Ballyferriter near Dingle, said that from his knowledge of the area the place where Ned claimed to gardai to have thrown the baby into the sea at Slea Head did not exist. He was sure our statements were true because basically we were all telling the same story. When it was pointed out to Detective Sergeant O'Donnell that only three of the statements referred to Dingle he replied, "I think three is a big amount." He said he was sure that if he were dumping a body his mind would not be at rest, he would be under a certain amount of pressure which would temper the description.

Detective Sergeant Kevin Dillon said he had received confidential information from a medical source which had led him to enquire about me from Garda Moloney and to interview Dr Creedon at Tralee General Hospital. He denied to the Tribunal that Dr Creedon had said that I had gone full term or near full term.

Detective Sergeant Dillon denied that any assault or battery or threats were made to Ned. These allegations were malicious and there was no truth in them, he said. When Ned had put his head in his hands before giving his statement there was something troubling him at that stage. He could not say why Ned, after more than an hour of denials, had suddenly changed his mind and given his statement.

He resented the media's linking of the case with the Shercock, County Cavan, case in which a man died in garda custody. "We have been charged, tried and convicted and it is only a matter of penalty," he noted at one stage. He also believed that the Minister for Justice was premature in comments he had made. A statement by Dublin TD Tony Gregory claiming that there was a conspiracy among the gardai had not been helpful either.

Regarding the dropping of the charges against us he said the Director of Public Prosecutions was disregarding the statements totally. He knew most of the gardai involved in the case. They were kind men and it was a privilege to work with them. None of them would condone ill-treatment in a garda station, he said.

Detective John O'Sullivan of Killarney was unlucky enough to catch the judge's wrath at the persistent garda assertion that they were not really investigating the murder of the Caherciveen baby when they went to our house on 1 May. The judge's anger seemed to grow as he made his point. He said that the gardai had had a suspect in South-west Kerry, a young unmarried girl who was known to have been pregnant and whose time was known to have gone by and who had not been seen around since the previous September. Enquiries had been made of doctors, hospitals, midwives and nurses and nobody knew of the delivery of her child. The gardai had gone to check her out and found that the child was there. The gardai had been investigating that lady for the Caherciveen baby, he said.

The judge then referred to me. Before 1 May the gardai knew that I had been in an advanced state of pregnancy and that I was no longer pregnant and that the child was not at our house. The gardai had gone to Garda Moloney in Abbeydorney who confirmed that I had been pregnant and that he had seen me a few days previously and that I was no longer pregnant. He had rung up Mary Shanahan, who told him that I had lost the baby in hospital. Mary Shanahan had told that to Garda Moloney with complete honesty because she had brought me to Dr Daly. The neighbours knew that I had been pregnant but was no longer pregnant. They believed that I had lost the baby in hospital, but the gardai knew that I had not.

"Yet you tell me and all of you tell me you go out to Joanne Hayes and are not really investigating the Caherciveen baby and I think that is a load of nonsense," the judge said. "The guards would have been failing in their duty if they did not have the gravest suspicions of Joanne Hayes to be the mother of the Caherciveen baby at that stage."

At the start of his intervention the judge had referred to the evidence of Auntie Aquinas. He said that he had spent a lot of time asking her about the fixation our family had of keeping the birth of my baby outside in the field rather than in the house. It was only fair to say that she had received undue publicity because of her evidence and he had reread her evidence and he was satisfied that she had endeavoured to give it truthfully and honestly as she knew the facts. Both sides seemed to be playing tennis or something, he remarked.

Detective Garda Michael Smith of Tralee said my mother had been treated with respect at all times. Referring to the allegation that he had told her that she was like a tinker on the road when he interviewed her on 1 May he said there was no way he would go into an old woman's house and start abusing her in front of a child still in nappies.

Garda Tim Collins of Dingle denied that he had been brought into the investigation because he was from Dingle and could introduce an element of local colour into the statements of Ned and Mike. He did not know of any place anywhere near Slea Head which fitted the descriptions of the place where Ned and Mike had indicated in their statements that they had thrown the baby into the sea.

He had not been asked until 2 May to investigate locally about the tides and currents in the area, he said.

The judge was impressed with this evidence and invited Dermot McCarthy to think about the matter over the weekend and said he might like to challenge the evidence. On Monday, Garda Collins remained emphatic that he was correct about the date.

Detective Garda Tim Mahoney denied that any pressure had

been put on Ned to make his statement and he believed everything that was in it. Did he believe that Ned had gone to Horan's garage on the other side of Tralee to get petrol on the way home from Slea Head! He did. Judge Lynch asked him why a man who had just completed a gruesome journey and who had only four and a half miles to drive home would drive a mile each way to get petrol when everyone was out and about. Detective Mahoney didn't know why.

I was small fry to Detective Sergeant Joseph Shelly. He had dealt with murderer Malcolm McArthur, among others, and he had been deeply impressed. McArthur, who had committed two murders, had offered to bring Detective Sergeant Shelly to the place where he said he had hidden the murder weapons but Detective Superintendent Courtney had refused the offer. Later McArthur had admitted that he would have done himself in if he had got the opportunity after being brought out. I too might have harmed myself if I had been brought out, according to the detective, although Superintendent Courtney had been on the point of bringing me out when the pair of them spoke at 7 p.m. on 1 May.

Kevin O'Higgins couldn't quite see the connection. McArthur had been in custody and had confessed. According to the gardai I was free to go and had been asking all day to brought to the field where I had said I had hidden my baby. Did he think I might try to drown myself in the pool of water? Detective Sergeant Shelly felt that the gardai would have lost out anyway. An hour later, he said, I "confessed".

Jeremiah had been reluctant to go home after being questioned at Tralee Garda station on 1 May, saying, "God, what am I going to tell my wife about all this?" Detective Sergeant Paul Downey of Killarney told the Tribunal. He denied that Jeremiah had asked to go home during the interview.

Jeremiah was quite frank about our relationship and Detective Sergeant Downey was satisfied after interviewing him that he was not involved. He had been the second suspect, after me, because he had the most to lose but he began to fade out of the picture as the interview progressed. "It was coming across to me that Locke was not the hot suspect that we thought he might have been," Detective Sergeant Downey said. He said that Jeremiah had been put through a searching interview but that no pressure had been put on him. He said that the fact that the gardai had ordered a blood sample to be taken from Jeremiah proved that there was no conspiracy on the part of the gardai. They already believed that the Caherciveen baby case had been solved but the blood test could confirm it or go against it. It indicated that the investigation was above board at that stage, he said.

Detective Sergeant Gerry O'Carroll and Sergeant P.J. Browne are both natives of Listowel, a Kerry town with the rare distinction of having contributed more to literature than Gaelic football. It is the home of Bryan McMahon and John B. Keane and the annual Writers Week festival. It is also the birthplace of Dr Louise McKenna, the forensic scientist.

Sergeant Browne was a Detective Garda in the Technical Branch at the time of the investigation but was now a Sergeant in the uniformed section in Cavan. He specialised in writing garda reports and was entrusted with compiling the file on our case. It became a celebrated document, a collector's item for the recipients of the eleven copies that were published. In its introduction he wrote: "Within the covers of this Garda Report and File is told a sad tale. It occurred because a young girl in her mid-twenties was scorned by the married man she loved, had children for and wanted for herself. 'Hell hath no fury like a woman scorned.'"

Detective Sergeant O'Carroll was observant. The first thing he noticed was my size. "She was very tiny. I don't know why that struck me but it did. She had her leg under her on the chair, she was sitting in a very odd position. She was birdlike in her appearance. She was edgy and nervous," he said. He had introduced himself and Detective Garda Browne and I chatted about where I lived and things like that. He had told me that they knew from the hospital authorities that I had given birth to a full-term baby and I had said that I had had a miscarriage and flushed it down the toilet. He had said that in that case they would find the foetus in the septic tank.

It was then, he said, that I cried for the first time and Detective Browne had told me to tell the truth about the baby. Almost straight away I had said, "I am a murderess, I killed my baby." That was less than ten minutes after their interview had commenced. He had immediately cautioned me. I had then described the birth of my baby in the field and told of disposing of it in the pool and I was very distressed as I spoke, weeping uncontrollably and moving around the room a lot. I would stare out the window vacantly as I spoke. During the account I had put my head over and cradled it into the shoulder of Detective Garda Browne who had put his hands around my shoulder.

I had cried and cried and afterwards Detective Garda Browne's shirt was stuck to him where I had cried. "It was a very sad sight. We tried to comfort her. At this stage she said she was insane. It was something she said a good bit during the day," Detective Sergeant O'Carroll told the Tribunal.

Without being insulting or hurtful, on that day he thought there was a little "want" in me. Having seen me at the Tribunal he had no doubt that I was a perfectly sane, logical girl but on that day he thought there was some little thing not completely right in me. Sergeant Browne was puzzled by me as well. During the interview I was at times very distraught and very upset and at times I was composed. That was one of the strange things about me, he said.

During those five and a half hours there had been no violence, no insults to me or to my family, no pressure on me. "If I ever find myself in a police station as a civilian I would love to be treated the way Joanne Hayes was treated," Sergeant Browne told the Tribunal.

Detective Sergeant O'Carroll said that prior to the second search he told Detective Superintendent Courtney that I was very convincing and he was sure the search would be successful. The relationship between us was cordial and sympathetic and we were calling each other Gerry, Joanne and P.J. but I became upset when I was told the second search revealed nothing. I then recounted the story that I had told earlier and insisted that the baby was out where I had said it was. He told me that while he believed that I had had a baby out on the land he now doubted the story of where the baby was.

Garda Moloney had come in at 7.55 p.m. and said he had been out on the search and they had found no baby and I had again given the same directions that I had been giving the detective. I had said, "Liam, it is out there." Seconds after Garda Moloney left Detective Garda Coote and Detective Garda Smith had come into the room. They had three articles with them: a plastic bag, a brown-handled carving knife and a long white plastic brush. Detective Sergeant Coote had told me that my mother had made a statement telling how the baby had been born in the room and

137

of the death of the infant and how it had been disposed of.

The plastic bag had been placed beside the chair and the knife and the brush on the table in front of me. I had become almost hysterical: very, very upset and very, very distressed, Detective Sergeant O'Carroll said. I had been asked to identify the objects and had made no reply. I was just overcome. Detective Sergeant Coote and Detective Garda Smith had then left the room.

I had identified the objects and began shouting that I was insane and that I had murdered my baby with the knife and bathbrush. He had again given me a legal caution. He was very surprised at these developments because he had been convinced by my demeanour that my previous statement had been correct. He asked me if I was telling the truth and I had indicated that I was.

"She had a way of composing herself which I found startling; she composed herself immediately. From then on she was very composed," Detective O'Carroll said.

From then on Detective Sergeant O'Carroll began writing as well. It was about 8.20 p.m.

Sergeant Browne denied vehemently that he had put me on his lap while the statement was being taken. On the one hand he was being accused of slapping me across the face and on the other that he had put me sitting on his lap.

He explained to Anthony Kennedy that he hadn't come straight out and told me that they were inquiring about the Caherciveen baby. He was conscious of my mental state that day, of my susceptibility to pressure or suggestions. "It is one of the fields I have a little more experience of than some of my colleagues. I lecture on sexual cases or rape or infanticide. The mental state of women who kill newborn infants is full of danger for susceptibility," he said.

He did not want to be facetious or hurtful but he believed that many children were being reared in homes all over Ireland where the father, or husband, was not the father. "We live in a promiscuous society. There have been umpteen cases of neighbours getting pregnant by their next door neighbour. It is happening, has happened and I'm basing it on that," he said. He had been asked to substantiate claims that I had been intimate with another man within forty-eight hours of having sex with Jeremiah Locke. No evidence had been produced but it could have happened, he said.

Was it his case that the alleged father of my alleged second child was one of my neighbours? Anything was possible. He would not like to cast aspersions on my neighbours, that would be a very unkind thing to do. All he was saying was that casual sex takes place. It doesn't have to be an affair, it doesn't have to last a night, it doesn't have to last an hour.

He still believed that the Caherciveen baby was mine. If I had not included the last four lines of my statement he would have had a far more open mind in the affair. I had said out of the blue, "When the baby was found in Caherciveen I knew deep down it was my baby." To him as an experienced detective, or indeed, as a human being there was a ring of truth to that that he could not deny.

"Regardless of how bad the conditions become," asked James Duggan, "you will continue to row into the eye of the storm?"

Detective Sergeant O'Carroll replied: "I will, yes."

Brian Curtin pointed out that I would have had to carry a weight of more than fourteen and a half pounds if I had had twins. Detective Sergeant O'Carroll said he was only a layman and could only express an opinion from what he knew himself. "Native Dublin women look hugely pregnant while a lot of country women do not look pregnant at all," he said.

Brian Curtin put it to Detective Sergeant O'Carroll that without reference to the statements there was no independent extrinsic evidence standing on its own to connect me with the Caherciveen baby.

"Yes, you are probably right," he said.

Kevin O'Higgins asked if it might have been very unsafe to take a statement from me at all given the huge variations in my mood. Detective Sergeant O'Carroll said it did cross his mind. He took more care with that statement; it lay unsigned for twenty minutes. He had had doubts about my mental condition that day and had given me every opportunity to deny it but I had eventually convinced him that I was telling the truth and he had been happy to let me put my name to the statement. He agreed with Judge Lynch that at the time I changed my story I was hysterical and that in such an hysterical condition I would be unlikely to be thinking of saving myself. Why then did I go back on my story of murdering the first baby if I had had twins?

"How often have I asked myself since that day in Tralee why did I not say to her, 'You are after having twins'."

James Duggan asked why the Twins Theory could not be dropped. Detective Sergeant O'Carroll said he thought that to do that at this stage would be to disregard so much evidence.

"Ye have thrown it in the air and ye might as well finish the game with it now. Is that it?"

"Yes."

Sergeant Browne told his counsel, Brendan Grogan that there had been a lot of playacting during my evidence. Kevin O'Higgins was interested in this observation. Did he not think this was a slightly unfair description? Sergeant Browne replied that shortly after leaving the Tribunal — within minutes — he had seen me surrounded by some ill-informed women journalists and I was very composed and happy and giggling. He did not agree that if my behaviour was "playacting" at the Tribunal it was "playacting" at the garda station, nor did he consider that his choice of phrase was unfortunate or ill-considered.

He insisted that there was no pressure on me when making my statement on 1 May. Did that mean that I had presented a brazen series of lies in my story to the Tribunal? Correct, Sergeant Browne said.

Judge Lynch had a question. Hadn't the sergeant said the previous day that I had expressed the wish to go when the searches proved unsuccessful and was I still quite happy not to go although the searches proved fruitless? Sergeant Browne said that I never expressed the wish to get out of the place.

Dermot McCarthy was interested in the sergeant's evidence to the garda inquiry. Sergeant Browne had told the chief superintendents that if I asked to be taken out to the farm once that was all. He was now recalling that I said it on a number of occasions.

His own counsel asked what he meant by writing in the report that while the possibility was that the Caherciveen baby was mine, the probability was that it was not. Sergeant Browne said that regarding the possibility, I had said that I had the baby in the room, that I had stabbed it, that it was a boy; it was also washed and Ned and Mike saw the Dingle patrol car. Ned said they used an 0-7-30 bag and there was an 0-7-30 bag found near the body. The probability was primarily because of the blood groupings results. As far as he understood, the grouping was an incontrovertible fact which ought to be brought to the attention of the readers of the file.

He said that on 19 September 1984 he and Detective Superintendent Courtney met the the Director of Public

Prosecutions Mr Eamon Barnes and a senior assistant Mr Simon O'Leary and Mr Barnes intimated that he was withdrawing the charges against me and the members of my family. Detective Superintendent Courtney asked the DPP what charge was being preferred against me in respect of the baby found on the land. He asked were they going to charge me with murder. The DPP said that my baby did not have a separate existence according to Dr Harbison.

"We were very, very surprised at that revelation," Sergeant Browne said. They had then asked if I would be charged with concealment and the director said there would be no charge. Sergeant Browne said that regardless of scientific opinion he still believed that I had twins and that my statements were true.

And the Azores Baby, could that be excluded?

"This is such a bizarre case that it is very hard to exclude anything," replied the segeant.

Experts

MY BODY WAS old hat by now. They wanted to know what made me tick. Anthony Kennedy, asked the judge to order me to submit to an examination by Dr Brian McCaffrey, psychiatrist. Judge Lynch said he couldn't grant the order, it would be up to me to agree. I refused but agreed to be examined by Dr John Fennelly again. We met on Friday 22 March at his rooms in Limerick on my way home from Dublin.

Dr Fennelly told the Tribunal that he had interviewed me for over an hour and a quarter. To me it had felt more like half an hour but I was on my way back to Yvonne again; I used to love Fridays for that reason. I regarded the examination as an assessment of my progress since we had met the previous May and nothing else. It never entered my head that everything I said or didn't say would be so important or that Anthony Kennedy would be waiting, medical textbooks in hand, to scavenge among the last morsels of my private self. He had slots for my behavioural patterns and medical terms to cover a multitude of whims.

Dr Fennelly told the Tribunal that I was now very well, I had no psychiatric symptoms and was not depressed. The Tribunal was a worry to me at times but when he saw me I was bright and cheerful and did not appear to be upset. My evidence was the same as it had been in prison and at the hospital. I was not very suggestible now. I had been depressed and guilty at our previous meetings and would have agreed to anything to get the interview over. I had told him that I had had no second baby, that I had been told that Yvonne would be put in an orphanage and that that was what forced me into signing the statement. He agreed that I might have been additionally put out because my first account of the events was not accepted, but when the baby was found in the field I had improved.

Dr Fennelly said I had expressed no sense of guilt or remorse towards Mrs Locke. Why in God's name didn't you? my friends asked afterwards. Because I wasn't asked, I said. Apparently I should have approached the examination with a well prepared strategy, remorseful and guilty, saying all the right things.

142

It was time to categorise. Anthony Kennedy and Dr Fennelly agreed that I was a sociopath, anti-social in behaviour and that I had a histrionic personality. I hadn't avoided the cameras outside the courtrooms so I was exhibitionistic and narcissistic. Was I frigid? No, Dr Fennelly had found that my affair with Jeremiah had been mutually satisfying.

There were fourteen elements to a histrionic personality and I had all of them. As it happened, half the population of Ireland had as well to a greater or lesser degree, Dr Fennelly told Kevin O'Higgins. The definitive histrionic personality comprised: superficial charm and average or superior intelligence; ability to be at ease in situations which would unsettle an average person; irresponsibility; shamelessness, a cavalier attitude to telling the truth; lack of regret for anti-social behaviour; poor judgement and failure to learn from experience; lack of insight; callousness, insincerity and incapacity for love and attachment; little response to kindness; no history of genuine suicide attempts; unrestrained and unconventional sex life; failure to have a life-plan, except to follow a consistent pattern of self-defeat; onset of sociopathic characteristics no later than in early twenties.

The doctor and the lawyers went through the various characteristics, awarding me merit marks as they saw fit. Dr Fennelly would award me a middle rating.

I began my own little game of categorising gardai and lawyers, the flamboyant, the verbose, the bullies. Was a man narcissistic because he changed his suit every day or exhibitionistic because he didn't go around smashing cameras? I had witnessed superficial charm and superior intelligence and people at ease in situations which would unsettle the average individual right in front of me in the witness box. There had been weeks of it, spectacularly highlighted by a cavalier attitude to telling the truth. Callousness? Too well I knew the pain that could cause.

I knew also that we would never get a psychiatric insight into the people I had in mind. Their sex lives wouldn't be probed nor would anybody seek out any possible extensions of their macho characteristics. It would be a brave psychiatrist who would do so and an expensive one.

Dr Brian McCaffrey decided to come along anyway at the invitation of the twenty-five gardai who were involved in the case. He felt very uncomfortable, he said because he hadn't examined me. He is Clinical Director of Psychiatry for the Eastern Health

Board and is attached to St Brendan's Hospital at Grangegorman in Dublin. My lawyers allowed me to give his evidence a miss.

It was apparently a new experience for Dr McCaffrey because he had never before given evidence about a person whom he had not met face to face. He agreed that it was an assessment rather than a diagnosis and was based on reading Dr Fennelly's evidence in Tralee, on hearing his evidence in Dublin, on reading Dr Fennelly's notes on me and the hospital notes on me and on watching me as I listened to Dr Fennelly. He had no reservations about his assessment, however, because he regularly made assessments from notes and from other doctors' observations.

My histrionic personality was, he said, shared by actresses who like to be noticed and we can have varying attitudes to sex. We can be not very interested in it, normally interested in it, very interested in it. I wondered when I heard this definition later if it caused some self-analysis among those who availed of the opportunity to hear Dr McCaffrey. Talk about covering a multitude!

Being the manipulative type I may have put one over on Dr Fennelly by getting myself transferred from jail to the hospital in Limerick, Dr McCaffrey said. My presentation of misery may have been mistaken for depression. The prison grapevine system would quickly let a newcomer know that if she claimed to be depressed she could get a transfer to a psychiatric hospital. He admitted that he had no evidence to show that I had spoken to other prisoners in Limerick.

Dr McCaffrey didn't think I was suggestible on the day of my interrogation. Suggestibility occurred most in people who were anxious and insecure, with no friends or support around them. Wouldn't I have felt pretty insecure in a garda station for the first time, being interrogated alone? I could have been, but not very, the psychiatrist told the judge.

Dermot McCarthy asked if since I had been told my child would be committed to an orphange and my mother taken to prison and the gardai had spent many hours talking to me about the Caherciveen baby, would these conditions not induce suggestibility? Dr McCaffrey didn't agree. He met many people charged with various offences who said that pressure had been brought on them to sign statements. In the vast majority of cases he didn't believe them.

He did not think that telling lies on oath would make any

difference to someone of my personality. Being a skilled manipulator with a personality disorder I had many of the characteristics of the histrionic individual and played the role of the victim or princess without realising it. I had managed to have myself cast in the role of victim, pushed around by the gardai and the courts and had become a major focus of attention. In fact, I played the role of victim perfectly. He had never seen anyone do it better. My playing of the role of princess arose in my relationship with Jeremiah. I had hopes of going off and living with him in total disregard for how I was going to be provided for and without any consideration for his wife and children.

He was not impressed by my letter to Liam Bohan. My expression of sorrow and remorse didn't strike him as being genuine but he did not think that I was trying to mislead Liam Bohan and he did not think it was manipulative in the sense that I was using it to help me get out of jail.

Kevin O'Higgins wasn't enamoured of Dr McCaffrey's assessment of my "acting" ability. He put it to the doctor that he had every reason to feel uncomfortable and suggested that his evidence had been rank speculation. (Throughout the Tribunal Mr O'Higgins gave the impression that of all the lawyers he would have been the first to declare that the king had no clothes.)

Dr Fennelly also examined Ned, Mike and Aunt Bridie in March. He found Ned to be of above average intelligence, a sensible, cute man, able to run a GAA club. He did not think he would be suggestible.

He examined Aunt Bridie in an office at Edenburn Hospital, Tralee. She was in a wheelchair and the hospital was for chronically ill old people. She was paralysed on the right side. Her physician had told him that she had cortical atrophy. She had been a heavy drinker and that might have been a factor in her illness. She had cerebro-vascular impairment and this affected the blood supply to the brain and reduced it. Her recent memory was poor but she would be quite lucid on longer term events. It was a senile state which was slowly developing and it was progressive over the last year or two.

She was quite clear on day and date but there were always little gaps. She could not think of what year it was. When he told her that he would be reporting to the Tribunal she was not interested. The nurses told him that she took no interest in the Tribunal. She did not read or look at television. Magazines were brought to her by our family and she did not read them. She looked into space and took no interest in anything. He had waited at one stage for four or five minutes to see if she would speak and she did not. He said that if he had waited for her to speak he would be still waiting.

She told him that she was quite happy and he thought her memory was good. In some ways her memory gaps were obvious but she stuck quite rigidly to the fact that the baby was born in the room. However, when he asked her what had happened to the baby she told him that the people from the funeral home came and took it.

Dr Fennelly said Aunt Bridie did not know the names of the nurses apart from Nurse Fitzgerald who told him that she was distantly related to her. He believed this was why she remembered the nurse's name. She was quite anxious to go home and felt my mother would look after her. He said we visited her regularly and I went to see her every weekend. There was no evidence that she had lost any contact with us over the previous month or so. She was sticking to the story as she had told it and was vague about some things. When he questioned her about her pension she could not remember how much it amounted to. From the point of view of suggestibility one could probably guide her to say things one wanted her to say.

Dr Fennelly said Mike would be easily influenced. He would be more easily manipulated than Aunt Bridie. Aunt Bridie had stuck to her substantive account but Mike showed an appreciable divergence. Regarding his evidence about the baby being born in the room he told Dr Fennelly that it did not happen and that he was not there. He also said he did not know anything about my baby until he was brought to the garda station. He made no bones about being poor in school. He could read a paper and that was about it. His first love was farming. He apparently owned the farm and Ned worked for him.

He denied saying anything about going to Slea Head with the baby's body and also said that he did not remember saying anything about my having a baby. He said he agreed with the gardai about the Caherciveen baby because he was nervous. It would be easy to get him to sign any statement, Dr Fennelly said, and added that his evidence would be most unreliable. It would be very difficult to determine the veracity of what he was saying and he had a high degree of suggestibility. He seemed to have little interest in the case as far as Dr Fennelly could see.

In January during the evidence of Dr Harbison and Dr McKenna we had noticed the distinguished looking man who was advising Messrs Kennedy in their cross-examinations. Somebody said his name was Dr Declan Gilsenan and he was a pathologist. On Friday 22 March he came back to take issue with his medical colleagues.

Tall, greying and sporting a David Niven-type moustache Dr Gilsenan oozed charm and confidence on the witness stand. At a table behind the lawyers Dr Harbison, Dr McKenna and Dr Maureen Smith of the National Forensic Science Laboratory took notes and occasionally handed bits of paper to Michael Moriarty and Kevin O'Higgins.

Dr Gilsenan, who is a pathologist with the Midland Health Board, said he was firmly of the opinion that our knife could have inflicted the injuries to the breast bone and heart. It was very likely that the injuries were caused by that sort of flat-bladed single-edge knife. Later he said there was nothing unique connecting the wounds to our knife.

Concerning the blood tests Dr Gilsenan said the chronology of what had happened to the specimens was important. He thought that the circumstances of transporting them to Dublin in Dr Harbison's car were not ideal. If Dr Harbison used the car heater at a comfortable sixty to sixty-five degrees it would have been a very adequate growth temperature for bacteria. Different bacteria produced different types of blood group-like substances and these were capable of contaminating tissues and red cells when they were in a liquid state so as to give false positive reactions with anti-serum.

He agreed with Dr McKenna that tissue samples were adequate for blood group purposes. He would have considerable doubt as to the validity and reliability of the blood groupings. He agreed with Dr McKenna that the Bombay Gene was not relevant in this case. He would find it difficult to exclude the brush as the instrument which had caused the injuries to the baby's head. The brush was not very heavy and would have to have been firmly wielded.

He was at a loss to explain the stab wounds other than the two on the breast bone. He wondered if they were post-mortem injuries inflicted by some kind of bird. Judge Lynch pointed out that the baby had been found face down, wedged firmly between two rocks. Therefore it would seem that birds of prey would not have had access to the front of the baby. The matter was of great importance because it had been suggested that I had stabbed the baby with a knife.

"Now we are introducing some other weapon of which we have heard no mention whatsoever up to this the fiftieth day of the inquiry," the judge said. "Where does that leave me?" he asked.

Dr Gilsenan suggested that a marine animal such as a squid could have caused the injuries. He would rule out a skewer, stiletto or bodkin-type weapon as having caused the centre-chest injuries.

Kevin O'Higgins put it to Dr Gilsenan that his views were largely based on speculation and had to be regarded as being extremely tentative. Dr Gilsenan replied that he had based his views on the history of the specimens as related by Dr Harbison and Dr McKenna. He told Michael Moriarty that he had stood in for Dr Harbison on seven or eight occasions and agreed that Dr Harbison had thirteen years experience as a forensic pathologist. He accepted that Dr Harbison had dealt with between two hundred and seventy-five and three hundred homicide cases and twenty to twenty-five cases of infanticide. He also accepted that Dr Harbison was more experienced and more highly qualified in forensic pathology.

As Dr Harbison left Dublin Castle he wore the satisfied look of a man who had seen and heard and conquered. He chatted amiably with journalists who waited around to request future interviews with him, then drove off to his lonely work. A man had been murdered in Cork and the gardai would be relying on his expert testimony in another courtroom. We wondered if they would be calling in Dr Gilsenan in that trial.

Dr Harbison was recalled to the witness stand on Monday 29 April. He said he had carried out experiments on umbilical cords in his laboratory. He was satisfied that it was possible for a women to break an umbilical cord with her hands if she had a good grip but he was certain beyond reasonable doubt that my baby's cord had been cut with a scissors, a knife or some such instrument.

He said that while the lung tissue of my baby showed evidence of expansion there was insufficient evidence to show that the baby had survived after birth. The presence of *vernix caseosa*, the cheesy substance which coats a new-born baby, suggested that it had not been washed. It would have been a very poor bit of washing if it was done at all, he said.

He said that Aunt Bridie's evidence was in some respects more consistent with the Caherciveen baby than with my baby. If asked which baby had survived for six hours and which had not he would have said the Caherciveen baby had. He would estimate the weight of the Caherciveen baby at about six to six and a half pounds and when pressed by Dermot McCarthy said it could have weighed as much as eight or nine pounds. He said there would have been much more penetration involved in the twenty-five lesser wounds on the Caherciveen baby if any degree of force had been used with a weapon such as a kitchen knife.

Dr John Creedon was recalled to give evidence and asked to speculate on how I would have looked if I were pregnant with twins weighing a total of over eleven and a half pounds weight, bearing in mind that Yvonne was eight pounds at birth. Dr Creedon said his colleague Dr Doyle had made a note that I had been quite large at the time of Yvonne's birth. Carrying twins weighing over eleven and a half pounds I would have looked very large, he said. I would have suffered from the problem of my centre of gravity being displaced. I would have been very distended and would have had considerable difficulty in getting around. I would have had a military bearing.

Professor Robert F. Harrison, associate professor of obstetrics and gynaecology at Trinity College, Dublin, said it was not possible to say whether an observer of a pregnant women would be more likely to observe that she would be larger if she were expecting twins. "If I am looking at somebody undressed and on the couch I get a clue earlier rather than later whether or not she is expecting twins," he said. Size was not a diagnostic feature with twins although he thought that the lay public would generally accept that a person was larger with twins.

James Duggan asked Professor Harrison if he had read Dr Creedon's evidence to the Tribunal and the professor replied tht he had tried to read nothing about the trial; he was almost a virgin there. If I had been pregnant with twins weighing more than eleven and a half pounds I would be more noticeable than with a single pregnancy. It was really speculation to say that I would have had a military bearing and that I would have had considerable difficulty in getting around. In obstetrics and gynaecology and in medicine generally nothing was black and white, it was all a grey area, Professor Harrison commented. Just like the law, all grey areas, the judge remarked.

The subject of black and white had come up in a different context earlier when Anthony Kennedy referred to a story in the *Daily Mirror* of 29 May 1978, concerning a West German woman of mixed racial background who had black and white twins by different fathers. Professor Harrison, who was one of the more flamboyant witnesses at the Tribunal, drew laughter from the gallery when he asked which page it was on. The woman had made love to a white West German and to a black American soldier on the same day. The twins had caused a medical sensation. I felt that it was another illustration of the pits which the gardai were prepared to dig to undermine what was left of my character.

Judge Lynch intervened to say that he presumed he should have great regard for the evidence of Garda Moloney to the effect that he spoke to me and endeavoured to get me to break off my relationship with Jeremiah Locke. That would have been sometime in the month of August 1983, exactly the time when my third pregnancy was conceived. The judge said he knew nothing about the circumstances of the women referred to by Mr Kennedy. "What sort of ladies are we dealing with? We don't know but we do know here," he said.

Dermot McCarthy asked if a woman of my weight and height and carrying twins would be able to continue working until the time of birth and Professor Harrison replied that every case was an individual one. Some women took to their beds while others carried on normally. "You don't have to be a cripple just because you are pregnant," he said.

Professor Harrison, who was seen to be wearing pyjamas beneath his clothing in the cafeteria during lunch, kept his audience on the edge of their seats throughout his evidence. At one stage he looked at his watch and asked if somebody would telephone his wife to tell her he would be late for their appointment and in one of the prize remarks of the entire Tribunal he said, "I have aunts who say someone is pregnant before they have intercourse."

Dr R.P. McCabe, a consultant marine engineer in Dublin, disagreed with Professor Barry's conclusion about the currents in Dingle Bay. He felt embarrassed in doing so, he said, but there was a zone of equilibrium in Dingle Bay and an object thrown in at Slea Head could indeed end up in Caherciveen. The currents were not northerly as Professor Barry had said and the admiralty charts used by the Professor were out of date.

I could never claim to be a militant feminist and I hope I am not being paranoid in suggesting that because Dr Louise McKenna is a woman her forensic findings came in for the severest challenge of all. Of course the blood groupings were crucial but there was still the nagging feeling that the male-dominated opposition believed that under pressure she would bow to her fallibility and retreat from her original unequivocal stand.

So they called Dr Patrick Lincoln, senior lecturer in serology at the University of London. Dr Lincoln is joint author of a number of books in the forensic sciences, is a paternity tester, a member of the Royal College of Pathology and a doctor of philosophy. The arrangement was that Dr Lincoln would perform tests on a sample of my blood at a Dublin laboratory. If I had given birth to an A group baby there would be some residues of A in my blood and the desperately necessary link to the Caherciveen baby would be established. If those A residues didn't show, Dr Lincoln would presumably be returned to London post haste.

But somebody on the Tribunal side, probably Judge Lynch we reckoned, felt that Dr Lincoln would be worth hearing in any case so the London doctor was served with a summons or subpoena when he arrived in Dublin on 9 May. A small balding man, he wasn't flamboyant or condescending in his highly technical evidence as some of the other medical men had been but showed instead a shy almost boyish eagerness to make himself understood in the plainest layman's language.

He listed some of his experiences in his gruesome work, including once putting together two halves of a body and finding that the two halves were different blood groups. (One half had been in water longer than the other.) But he had found no evidence at all of the precious A type in my blood. If he had been faced with the test on the Caherciveen baby he would have repeated the test because it was crucial. He would have performed two tests and he quoted a paper by Dr Margaret Perrera and pointed out that Dr McKenna had only done one type of test.

Michael Moriarty asked Dr Lincoln about the issue of twins by different fathers — super-fecundation as it was being called now in the Tribunal. The doctor said it was exceedingly rare, so rare that one ruled it out.

Next morning Dr McKenna took the stand again. Sitting in the public seats beforehand she had looked enviably relaxed as she chatted with a friend. For a lady whose professional reputation was on the line she seemed almost unconcerned. We soon discovered why. She hadn't done just one repeat test on the tissue from the

Caherciveen baby, she had done three. In the four tests three had shown no trade of O and the second of the tests had shown a trace of O. She stood over her blood groupings and said she was satisfied beyond doubt that I was blood group O and the Caherciveen baby was group A. She also quoted from a paper by Dr Margaret Perrera which stated that the second test, which she had not done, would have been unreliable in the case of the Caherciveen baby.

Dr McKenna had also sent all her samples to Dr Joseph Corr, chief paternity tester in Northern Ireland, and he had concluded that Jeremiah could not have been the father of the Caherciveen baby, not only on the basis of blood type but of the genetic characteristics CB which were in the baby's blood. Only two per cent of the population shared those blood type and genetic characteristics. Even if the blood typing was wrong, which he said he was not suggesting, and the correct group was O, could Jeremiah contribute the CB characteristics to the Caherciveen baby?, Judge Lynch asked. Dr McKenna said he could not.

The judge gave the lawyers permission to re-examine. Paul Gallagher had a last try, speculating about bacterial contamination of the CB enzymes, but it was a non-starter. Bacteria don't mimic enzymes, Dr McKenna said. She stepped down, the only female winner at the Tribunal. She hadn't shown any sign of resentment at being challenged nor was she intolerant of irrelevant questions, although she did tell Mr Gallagher on one occasion that his question was unfair in the scientific sense. She was an impeccable witness, a magazine noted later.

Subsequently, Dr Corr confirmed that on the basis of his findings Jeremiah could not be the father of the Caherciveen baby and I could not be the mother if I was not involved with any other man. A London genetic expert, Dr David Hopkinson, expressed reservations about the blood groupings but reservations were hardly enough now.

Dr McKenna had stood the test.

John Courtney

HE WALKED BRISKLY up the right-hand side of the hall, head tilted slightly forward, eyes fixed firmly on the chair, jaw cocked like an unwilling racehorse. It was 3.25 p.m. on 8 May and for Detective Superintendent John Courtney the long wait since 7 January was over. The public area was buzzing as the man in the navy suit and spotlessly white shirt took his seat. Some had come to see and hear but you didn't have to be a mindreader to know that there were those who hoped to see him sizzle or even fry. Detective Superintendent Courtney had left some indelible memories during his controversial career.

In the witness box he managed to be distinctive without being stylish. He is Kerry to the core. He talked of dates in "Aypurel" and referred to me as being "unmarrad". Similarity became "similiarity" and killed was pronounced "kilt". Most revealing was his persistence over three days in calling me Johanna. My brother Mike calls me Joanne but his statement of 1 May is full of Johanna and Detective Superintendent Courtney spent more than two hours with Mike that day.

He was unhappy in the box, scarcely concealing his anger at being called on to account for himself. A man of action rather than words, that high, wrinkled forehead hid a million secrets. He had been in the garda force for thirty-seven years and superintendent for seven. The anger was evident from the way he turned away from the lawyers when he answered questions and by his failure to add "My Lord" as the other garda witnesses had parroted at the end of each answer.

He told of investigating more than a hundred murders and he had led the searches for kidnap victims Dr Tiede Herrema and Don Tidey. He mentioned his long experience at every opportunity. He had investigated more murders, conducted more searches and seen more dead bodies than anyone in the force and he still hated seeing corpses.

He had taken over from Detective Sergeant Shelly in the Caherciveen baby case when developments had switched to me. He had heard of this girl of loose morals who had been pregnant and inquiries at hospitals and elsewhere had failed to locate a baby as a result of that pregnancy.

He had met me in a room at the station while I was being interviewed by Garda Moloney and Ban Gharda O'Regan and he had introduced himself and told me that he was inquiring into the recent birth of a baby to me. I had been looking out the window and struck him as being calm and relaxed. He had told me that it was hard to believe my account of giving birth outside in the field alone. I had told him of disposing of the baby's body in a stream near the house. I had said it was one field away from the house, near an old bedstead and he had said he didn't believe my story. He had asked me was it the afterbirth I had put in the pool and I had said, "No, it was the baby."

He denied that he had pointed his finger into my shoulder. He said he pointed his finger towards me and agreed that he told me a number of times to tell the truth. He said he did not discount my story. He was puzzled but still said it could have happened.

It was serious stuff but Martin Kennedy managed to draw a laugh all the same. Detective Superintendent Courtney had again denied pointing his finger into my shoulder. "Have you ever touched a woman in your life?" asked Martin Kennedy.

"No, my Lord, not in that regard anyway."

Although he covered his mouth with a hand James Duggan couldn't conceal his reaction. His dancing eyes and quivering shoulders gave him away. He wasn't the only one struggling to stay serious. Minutes later we almost lost our witness when a leg of his chair slipped over the edge of the little platform which supported the witness stand, but the ever vigilant Martin Kennedy saw the danger and saved the day.

Detective Superintendent Courtney told Mr Kennedy that there was no truth at all in the suggestion that he had organised the making up of statements by our family. Neither had there been any conference on 1 May to bring together information from the various statements. He said that at all stages he believed that I should be charged with infanticide and not murder, but he later learned that a murder charge had to be brought first with the possibility of reducing it to infanticide. Nothing had occurred on 1, 2 or 3 May to cast any doubt on our statements.

When my baby was found he thought that I had given birth to twins and he still believed it, going by the facts in the statements. He admitted that the forensic evidence cast a doubt but he still believed that I was the mother of the Caherciveen baby. He had been involved in the investigation of the Captain Nairac case in which a person had been charged with his murder although his body had not been found and going on our statements I too could have been charged even if my baby had not been found.

On the morning of 9 May Detective Superintendent Courtney was approached by RTE journalist Joe O'Brien who asked him if he would mind going outside for a moment so that the television cameraman could get a new picture of him. Mr Courtney agreed and the deed was done in a minute or two. I am not for a moment suggesting that Detective Superintendent Courtney enjoyed being photographed but it is worth pointing out that nobody labelled him an extrovert for doing so or speculated about whether he was exhibitionistic or histrionic.

Detective Superintendent Courtney rejected the suggestion that the searches on our farm on 1 May were half-hearted. "When I do a search I do a thorough search," he said.

To him it was just another case, he wasn't excited over it at all. Jeremiah had been eliminated at three or four o'clock when Detective Sergeant O'Donnell said he wasn't involved. Why was he detained for over three hours after making his statement, Dermot McCarthy asked. Detective Superintendent Courtney wouldn't accept that he had been detained. If he had got up at any time and said he wanted to go he'd have been free to go, he said.

He had spent considerable time with Mike and neither he nor Detective Sergeant Shelley had laid a hand on him. He could not have grabbed Mike by the collar of his jacket because he was not wearing a jacket. He was wearing a green pullover and he couldn't have stared at him because Mike kept looking at the ground. He couldn't get any reliable information from Mike because Mike was constantly switching from a baby to Yvonne and contradicting himself. They had spoken about farmwork, cows, hobbies and had a general conversation.

He thought it was at about 5.30 p.m. that Detective Sergeant O'Carroll told him that I "had expressed a willingness" to go out to the farm. Dermot McCarthy pointed out that O'Carroll had put the time at 2.45 p.m. Courtney said he wasn't saying that the detective was wrong but he thought he had been given that information at 5.30. He never told the searchers to search two hundred yards from the house because he didn't recall being told that. He blamed me for not being precise in my directions. If I had told Garda Moloney precisely where it was they would have found the baby if it was there. He didn't know there was a bedstead there, he had never been on our farm in his life.

Kevin O'Higgins suggested that it was the most spectacularly unsuccessful search he had ever conducted.

Dermot McCarthy put it to the witness that I had never changed my account of where the baby was. "Wasn't I speaking to her, don't I know better?" Detective Superintendent Courtney replied angrily.

When the search failed he decided to bring me to the farm. It was around 7 o'clock and he was sitting alone in his office, his back to the wall. Up to then he had hesitated because he didn't know what mental effect it might have on me. The baby's body could have been mutilated by vermin and it could have been the cause of a breakdown in my health and he would have had it on his conscience for the rest of his life. Women's minds were peculiar after giving birth, he said.

He had fully intended bringing "that women" out to the farm but then at about 7.30 Detectives Smith and Coote arrived in his office and Coote read him a statement in which my mother said that I had killed a baby with a bathbrush. The detectives had the bathbrush, a knife and a bag with them. Now he had three people saying that I had murdered a baby and that the baby was gone from the farm. (Ned and Mike had "confessed" during the afternoon but their statements weren't completed until much later.) He told the detectives to put Mom's statement to me and to show me the bathbrush, the knife and the bag. He agreed that Mom had made no reference to the knife but the three things were together and he asked them to show me the lot. What he was really interested in was the bathbrush, he said. He was convinced by my mother's statement and he remained convinced to this day, he said.

At around 9 o'clock he was told that Kathleen had made a statement saying that I was responsible for the baby's death and at about the same time Detective Garda Browne told him that I had made a statement admitting that I had killed a baby. He then had a discussion with Superintendent O'Sullivan and they called in Mr Donal Browne, the State Solicitor. Mr Browne studied all the statements and talked to the gardai involved.

Detective Superintendent Courtney was quite satisfied that a baby was born in the house, had been killed in the house and had been disposed of. As far as he was concerned the substance of the statements was true. In all his years investigating murders he had never heard a person tell the full truth in a statement.

At 7 o'clock the next day he heard about the finding of my baby. Did that not throw a doubt on the statements? He said his reaction was that I had given birth to twins. There had been no scepticism or reservations among the gardai and nobody had come to him to say otherwise. He said it never struck him as strange that I had never referred to twins in my long statement. He was satisfied that we knew quite well that we were free to leave the garda station. But hadn't I wanted to go home? Dermot McCarthy asked.

"She wanted to go out to the land to show where her baby was. That's a different thing altogether," he replied.

He said that at the post mortem Dr Harbison had not been able to give a definite statment as to the cause of death, but he had said that the baby had a separate existence. Asked what had been his reaction when he heard about the blood groupings Detective Superintendent Courtney said he had had none whatsoever. He didn't question Dr McKenna's findings. Did the findings not shake his faith in twins? No. He was satisfied that I had had a baby in the field and a second baby in the house. How did he explain Dr McKenna's findings? He knew that apparently I was of loose morals and he could not rule out the possibility that I had been intimate with some other man. He had never at any time said he was satisfied that I was the mother of the Caherciveen baby. What he had said was that the baby that had floated across the bay to An Trá Bán (The White Strand) could have been mine.

Were the charges against us related to the Caherciveen baby? Mr Courtney said he thought they were, yes. Pressed by Dermot McCarthy he said the forensic evidence had cast some doubt on my being the mother of the Caherciveen baby. There was a possibility that there were two babies floating in the waters of Dingle Bay, a remote possibility.

Why was it so important to the gardai that there should be twins in this case, asked Dermot McCarthy.

Because there were two babies, one at home and the other at Caherciveen, replied Detective Superintendent Courtney.

And two mothers, I wanted to scream.

He did not agree with the decision to drop the charges against me but he accepted it as it was the function of the law officers in the Director of Public Prosecutions' office to make decisions on the basis of reports which he submitted to them.

Final Stages

DONAL BROWNE, THE State Solicitor for Kerry, set the tone for his evidence within a minute of taking the oath. "You have an extensive private practice as well," suggested James Duggan. "That's debatable," replied Mr Browne. It was to be an on-the-level contribution, straight from the shoulder. Even the judge's face lit up at the prospect.

Mr Browne recalled that on the night of 1 May 1984 he had been at home watching television at about 9.45 or 10 o'clock when he received a phone call requesting him to go to Tralee garda station. He met Detective Superintendent Courtney and Superintendent Donal O'Sullivan and they told him evidence had come to hand which they wished to discuss with him. He read my statement and talked to Detective Sergeant Dillon who was taking Ned's statement and to Garda Moloney who was with Kathleen. He was told what was basically in their statements and in my mother's. He had a general discussion with the two superintendents and they appeared to agree that there were grounds for a charge of infanticide against me and of concealment against the others. He then found he was constrained to prefer a murder charge against me but felt that that would later probably be reduced to a charge of infanticide, subject to psychiatric evidence.

Mr Browne said that in a way he was more concerned with Kathleen because it seemed she was more at risk than any of us. If her evidence was correct she could have assisted in carrying out a murder. She would have supplied the murder weapon and could have been an accessory before the fact. She could have ended up in prison for murder. He decided not to prefer a murder charge against her but to present the facts to the Director of Public Prosecutions. He would charge her with the comparatively minor offence of concealment for the moment. He decided not to charge my mother then on compassionate grounds. "She wasn't going to leave the jurisdiction at her age," he said.

He said that while he was in the superintendent's office he noticed a map of Kerry on the wall behind Superintendent O'Sullivan's chair. He had pointed to the map to show the route the baby would have had to travel from Slea Head to Caherciveen and he told the superintendents that they would need to find out about the prevailing winds and the tides. In direct contradiction of Garda Collins's evidence they said they had already checked them out. He had also remarked that they should inquire if the patrol car had been out early that morning. "It was I who raised the topic of the winds and tides. I hopped the ball," Mr Browne told Dermot McCarthy.

It was Superintendent O'Sullivan who phoned him to tell him about the finding of my baby in Abbeydorney. This greatly complicated the case. He phoned the office of the Director of Public Prosecutions and reported the finding of my baby and he reread the statements.

On 31 May Detective Superintendent Courtney and Superintendent O'Sullivan met him at his office for about an hour and a half. "They were very concerned and indeed so was I," Mr Browne said. By then the blood groupings had been ascertained. They went over the statements again and Mr Courtney wanted to know what Mr Browne thought about it. Detective Superintendent Courtney still believed that I had murdered the child in Caherciveen. Mr Browne's view, which he expressed to the two superintendents, was that the onus was on the state to sustain the charges beyond reasonable doubt and in the absence of any contradictory evidence Dr McKenna's findings would have to be accepted. "I haven't seen any contradictory evidence to this day," he said. "When Mr Courtney was wondering if the blood groupings were correct and if there had been a mistake I said, look, you have to accept the facts. I think he had some doubt about it," Mr Browne added.

As far as Mr Browne was concerned the charges preferred on 1 May were dealing with the baby found in Caherciveen, "even if there were ten more babies." Detective Superintendent Courtney took the view that I had given birth to both babies and as far as Mr Browne could remember Superintendent O'Sullivan agreed.

How did the Twins Theory impress Mr Browne? "Not greatly. I took that with a grain of salt. I think Detective Superintendent Courtney genuinely believed that." He added, "Maybe I was crazy to put the charges first day but I stand over them and accept responsibility for them on the evidence that was before me on 1 May."

He said he discussed the case with Mr Simon O'Leary from the office of the Director of Public Prosecutions on a number of occasions and then Mr O'Leary wrote to him about "this crazy case" and told him to drop it fast. "I was glad to get out of it, as far as I was concerned that was the end of the saga," he said amidst laughter in various parts of the hall.

He agreed again that the charges referred to the Caherciveen baby: "It's only rubbish to suggest otherwise."

He agreed he had not read Kathleen's or Mike's statements that night but he knew the gardai who were taking them and he regarded them as very efficient. "There are some members of the gardai who have their own way of taking statements but I believe Liam Moloney wouldn't put a hand on anybody and I believe what that man said."

Regarding the winds and tides, he had told the superintendents to check them and they could check with the local blacksmith for all he knew.

He told Dermot McCarthy that the question of the blood groupings changed the whole complexion of the case. It had been a very important factor in his conversation with the superintendents. One had to get back to basics. He accepted the statements at their face value at the time. If he had the statements and read them every night up to Christmas he'd have come to the same decision.

"If I'm nothing else I'm decisive. If today was yesterday and I was back in the garda station I'd do the same again. If you can't make up your mind you shouldn't be in the job at all." If he were given a brief to prove twins with different blood groups he'd hand it to a barrister and tell him to look after it for him and get out of court as fast as he could.

"I'm not Sherlock Holmes. I'm a poor ignorant country prosecutor down in the mountains of Kerry trying to do my incompetent best. What do you think I am, a magician?"

Magician or not, Mr Browne had gone a long way towards putting things in perspective. Unlike so many other witnesses he didn't claim infallibility or deny that he may have made a mistake. He had felt justified originally but had been prepared to face the facts as they emerged.

If there had been one or two men of his calibre on the garda side there need never have been a Tribunal.

Pat O'Shea is a mortician at Tralee General Hospital. He remembers the post mortem on my baby because it was his first forensic post mortem and also because of the unusually large number of gardai who attended. He told the Tribunal that Dr Harbison told those present that he had not established whether the baby had a separate existence. He did not recall Dr Harbison saying, "Gentlemen, we have a separate existence."

In the course of his duties he meets many gardai and he felt that he was on good terms with them. He also comes from a family of staunch republicans but he has never take an active part in politics. His life centres around his Northampton-born wife Susan (Foley) and their young children Sean and Tina.

He was totally unprepared for the attitude of Anthony Kennedy. Mr Kennedy put it to Pat that his house had been searched and that he had been questioned by gardai in connection with the kidnapping of supermarket executive Don Tidey and about a robbery in Kenmare. Pat admitted that his house had been searched once but repeatedly denied that he had ever been involved in a political organisation and said he resented these things being thrown at him.

Dermot McCarthy intervened to ask if such issues were relevant but Judge Lynch said it was relevant to ascertain whether the witness had a grudge against the gardai. Pat said that many gardai present would tell Mr Kennedy that he had nothing to do with political organisations and the lawyer replied that he had spoken to his clients and that was why he was questioning him on those matters.

"Would you not use this opportunity to slag the guards if you could?" Mr Kennedy asked.

"I would not. I have always co-operated with the guards and I resent it being thrown back in my face," Pat O'Shea replied. He denied that he had attended H-Block demonstrations or that he frequented such company. He agreed that a van was found on his mother's farm bearing the number plate of a taxi after both taxi and van were stolen in Dublin. He pointed out that he did not live there, he lived in his own house a half a mile away. He did not know anything about the taxi having been used in a Kenmare robbery, nor did he know anything about a parking sign which was stolen from an ambulance in Tralee hospital and later used by the car involved in the Tidey kidnapping. He told Michael Moriarty that he had never been charged with a criminal offence.

He became involved in the Tribunal because Patrick Mann had got his name at the hospital as having assisted Dr Harbison at the post mortem. He had made a verbal statement to Patrick Mann and a week later Patrick had returned with the statement typed out and had asked him to read it and see if he was happy with it. He had done so and signed it. Anthony Kennedy asked Pat to spell three words from the statement and when Pat mis-spelt them Mr Kennedy suggested that Pat had not had much input into the statement.

Later that evening on the train from Dublin, Pat was very hurt by the way he had been treated at the Tribunal. He had not asked or volunteered to give evidence and he felt he had been insulted without any justification. He described what had happened on the one and only occasion that his house was searched. It happened at about 9 o'clock in the morning as Pat was feeding Sean, who was then only fifteen months old. Pat's wife was in hospital at the time and he was going to take the child to his mother's house for the day while he would be at work. Some gardai arrived at his house and two came in. He knew one of them, Detective Dan Kelliher who was an official of the Credit Union, and he offered him a cup of tea. Detective Kelliher declined the offer, saying he was in a hurry. Pat provided a stool for the gardai to enable them to look up in the attic and they were gone again inside of a couple of minutes.

"It was the only time they ever raided my house. They asked no questions and I didn't ask any. I've never in my life been questioned about republican activities. If they did suspect me why didn't they question me?" Pat wondered.

On the day prior to his testimony the gardai had given him £30 to cover his fare to Dublin. The actual fare was 50 pence more and Pat estimated that his trip cost him an additional £26 pounds in expenses.

It wasn't easy to evaluate his disillusionment.

With the exception of a crew from Thames Television who were working on a programme called *TV Eye,* and a photographer for a local newspaper, *Kerry's Eye,* all the members of the media with whom we came in contact treated us very fairly. From the start we were open and frank with the reporters who told us later that they were surprised initially to find that we were so accessible and so willing to co-operate. We allowed them to read our letters and cards and when I received Valentine cards they saw them too and quoted from them in their newspapers.

Thus news of the marriage proposals I received found their way into the news and we had little privacy, but I believe that because we were so open in our dealings with them the reporters felt obliged to reciprocate and none of them ever tried to take us unawares or to put an unfair slant on anything we did or said.

That is not to say that we weren't often annoyed that we seemed always to be making the headlines. Even when the gardai were under pressure in the witness box and things seemed to be going well for us the headlines in the papers were invariably about us, thanks to some allegation or speculation by a garda. The reporters explained to us that they weren't responsible for writing the headlines and they were often embarrassed when we protested to them.

It seemed paradoxical that during my cross-examination, in particular, the papers were commenting editorially about counsels' insensitive approach to their task and at the same time were carrying all the intimate detail in their reports on other pages of the same editions.

Deirdre Purcell's summaries in the *Sunday Tribune* were relished in our area because she always managed to reconstruct the week's events with uncanny perception and objectivity. She made a point of steering clear of both sides in the affair, apart from occasionally asking one of us to clarify something for her, and she had no hesitation in pointing to a loophole wherever she saw one, regardless of whose toes she stepped on.

Nell McCafferty was quick to throw her full weight against what she saw as a male chauvinist steamroller crushing the defenceless with the full backing of the system and she never pretended to be anything less than totally behind us, at least in principle.

Gene Kerrigan's wrap-up report in *Magill* magazine at the end of the Tribunal was a masterly effort and was widely read. He too had persistently avoided any close contact with us and presented the relevant details as he saw them in a fair and unbiased review of the case.

Unfortunately, we have nothing but bitter memories of the visit of the Thames Television crew, who for a couple of weeks made our lives a misery. Initially they refused to accept that under the judge's rulings concerning contempt we simply could not be interviewed by them even if we had wished to, but it was when they arrived in Kerry that they became really intrusive. One Sunday we went to mass at Kilflynn because one of their cars was parked near the church in Abbeydorney and the following weekend they kept us literally hemmed in our house while they took up position on the road. We missed mass on the Sunday before St Patrick's Day as a result and another day we put No Trespass signs at the entrance to our house but they drove by them into our yard. John Barrett had a difficult time persuading them that they were not welcome.

They warned him that they were very patient people and that they would "get" us and of course they did. From the road they managed to "capture" Mom on film in our kitchen and once they got into action in Dublin Castle we had no escape. If they had been a little more understanding at the outset we would have been as co-operative as possible, at least to the extent of allowing them to film around the farm as we had done for a very courteous crew from Channel Four a couple of weeks earlier. In the event the Thames Television programme was quite fair, as we discovered to our relief when somebody showed us a video recording later.

Much was made of our willingness to co-operate with photographers, especially by Anthony Kennedy who in his probings for psychiatric labels that could be fastened on to me was at pains to emphasise narcissism and exhibitionism. The truth was that where the photographers were concerned it was a matter of accepting the inevitable fact that there were no secret passages out of the Tribunal locations and there could be no escape. We used to simply keep walking while they filmed and the fact that we were often caught smiling was because we got to know these lads and they usually managed to draw a laugh from us, even by calling themselves all kinds of nuisances. There would have been absolutely no point in trying to run or to cover our faces; that would have been the picture they all wanted.

Towards the end of the Tribunal I began to yield to both the mental and physical pressure. The travelling to and from Dublin, the absences from home and from Yvonne especially, and the unvarying routines between hotel and Tribunal left me exhausted and it took me a few weeks afterwards to recover.

In my life up to 1 May 1984 I had had little contact with the gardai or the law. I knew a few of them as patrons of the sports centre and they had touched my life only to the slightest extent through my Uncle Maurice's position as a peace commissioner. Our local garda in Abbeydorney, Liam Moloney, had been a friendly presence in the community, often operating more as a social worker of sorts than as an enforcer of the law. He had been acting in that characteristic role in speaking to me in 1983 about my relationship with Jeremiah Locke.

I had never had any occasion to question the behaviour of the gardai in general or of any particular garda. I read in newspapers and heard and saw radio and television coverage about allegations of garda methods but I just thought that the allegations came from subversive and criminal elements and they made no impression on me. I always believed the garda version in such cases.

As for the law, I had never been in any court, none of my family had ever been charged with anything, apart from Ned's conviction for drunken driving, and if I thought about it at all I suppose I assumed that people got the treatment they deserved and got justice in the courts.

My experience in Tralee garda station on 1 May 1984 came as a complete shock to me and it was immediately followed by the experiences of prison and psychiatric hospital. As I tried to get back to some kind of normality at home prior to my first court appearance, and again after the charges were dropped, I was confused, puzzled and upset and I tried to absorb the content of what was being said about me and about the gardai in the newspapers and on radio and television.

In approaching the Tribunal I knew almost nothing about the way in which courts, let alone tribunals, operated, and I was utterly unprepared for what happened.

As the Tribunal began to settle into its probing concentration on my personal and sexual life I felt bewildered and horrified. What had been announced as an enquiry into the behaviour of the gardai had already become, even before I gave evidence, an inquisition into my life and character.

Although I have been a member of the Fianna Fail party since I was about sixteen I had never really considered questions of power and how it is structured; I had never considered the law as such and how it operated within society. But as I looked at many of the lawyers and heard their accents and tones of voice, I felt as if they were some kind of alien force — alien, that is, to the society in which I had lived. In their manners and in the ways they spoke they seemed to be expressing some kind of code which I had never encountered before and as the Tribunal progressed I grew to hate that code.

I suppose that in my upbringing there were always some basic rules of decency and humanity. They weren't really spelled out at all, though of course there were sermons by priests and talks by nuns at school which made various statements about morality and so on, but it was more or less taken for granted that there were certain ways you behaved towards other people and certain ways you did not. Whatever system of values the legal process of the Tribunal was operating under it didn't seem to have anything in common with the kind of values that I had taken for granted and that were part of the society from which I came.

In our religion the priests allow for their humanity by telling us to do what they say and not specifically what they do. Human frailty is conceded among the clergy in doctrine, at least, but never among the lawyers. They score off your inability to express yourself and cash in on your inexperience. Seizing on an intellectual advantage over another human being in a court of justice cannot be moral, but it is legal.

I knew nothing about giving evidence but I learned as the proceedings went on that there are some ways of giving evidence that go down well and other ways that do not. I was floundering for most of the five days of my inquisition and I contrasted badly with the practised and studied approach of the gardai, who had of course given evidence many times before and whose business was so closely linked with the law courts. But I suppose what struck me most was that there seemed to be no humanity in the relentless way in which I was pursued by my legal interrogators. The process of the law allowed for me to be torn asunder and every part of me examined in such a way as to denigrate and degrade me. Small wonder, then, that I began to ask myself why this should be, and for what purpose.

Members of the gardai and their behaviour were supposed to be under investigation, but instead what was not only investigated in questioning, but chewed over and held up for disapproval, was my character and the character of my family. It was as if I had to be punished for the crime of embarrassing the gardai, and the means of that punishment was the legal process of inquisition.

The intense media attention focused on the Tribunal and on me meant, among other things, that I came into contact with people from very different backgrounds from my own who were used to taking particular views about society, the law, the role of women in society, and the state. I had never attached much meaning to the words "the system" but as I tried to make sense of what I was experiencing, as I heard the comments around me, and as I read the newspapers, I came to feel that what I was up against and what was presiding over my torture was something you could call "the system".

God knows, I'm no angel and I'm certainly no heroine either, but I was engaged in an unequal battle which I couldn't have won even if I was both of those things, and when I broke down it was just the inevitable result of the pressure put on me.

Some people from civil liberties groups and so on suggested that my case was typical of many cases in which the gardai succeeded in getting confessions from innocent people. I don't know whether that is true; before 1 May 1984 I could never have believed the gardai could or would make anyone sign a false statement; now all I know is what happened to us and that makes me think that similar events have taken place in other cases.

During the Tribunal I received a nice letter from Nicky Kelly whose treatment by the law is generally regarded as the most notable story of injustice in Ireland in recent years. In the words of "The Wicklow Boy", Christy Moore's song about him,

> Seven years ago his torture started,
> A forced confession he was made to sign.
> Young Irish men specially trained and chosen
> Were on the Heavy Gang that made him run the line.

When I met him, quite by accident in Dublin, I felt a kind of fellowship with him because he knew from experience what it was like to encounter the Heavy Gang.

Feminists have said that the Tribunal showed that the legal system and the whole system of power in Irish society is male-dominated. Poor Marguerite Egan, a member of the Tralee Women's Group, got short shrift from Judge Lynch when she tried to hand in a letter to the Tribunal during the final week of the Tribunal. The judge was rising for lunch and Marguerite wasn't interfering with the morning's work. Neither was she attempting to make a submission on my behalf (indeed, I knew nothing in advance about her gesture); she merely wished to express a viewpoint from a representative group about how women are treated in court, not just me, but women in rape cases, but the response she got was that she must sit down and have sense or go to jail for contempt.

Women's groups have accused the Church of hypocrisy. Certainly I felt I was some kind of prey pursued by hunters, who were men and who invaded the privacy of my body and my emotions in their dragging out of all the details about me. My main tormentor was a pillar of the Church.

The process of coming to terms with my experience at the hands of the law is still going on, but whatever conclusions I come to they are far from the naive and ignorant trust I felt before 1 May 1984.

Predictably, the submissions by lawyers which commenced on 10 June and lasted five days amounted to a packaging of the humiliating questions that had been the pattern during the preceding five months. Anthony Kennedy said I was a self-confessed, compulsive liar; Ned's credibility had been severely challenged; and Mom was "a pathetic woman who was reduced to calling her son Mike a perjurer and even her sister, Bridie."

Martin Kennedy said that in a force of eleven thousand four hundred gardai there must be some bad apples, but ninety-nine point nine per cent of the gardai had pride in their jobs. He described us as the most discredited family in the country.

Dermot McCarthy suggested that if the gardai had turned around on 3 May 1984 and admitted that something had gone wrong with their case this Tribunal would not have been held. However, the gardai had tried to justify their actions and this must throw doubts on their bona fides. The intensity of my relationship with Jeremiah Locke was such that it excluded me having a parallel relationship with another man and no evidence was produced to this effect.

Kevin O'Higgins said an issue which existed in the public mind and which had dissipated somewhat since was whether the gardai in some way were not willing or anxious to abide by the decision of the Director of Public Prosecutions to drop the charges. Of course nothing could be further from the truth, he said. It was blindingly obvious that I had been charged with the murder of the Caherciveen baby and no other, he said, but then the gardai had retreated to some extent to the possibility of a third baby.

Mr O'Higgins, quoting James Thurber, said: "We live man and worm in an age where almost anything can mean almost everything because this is the age of gobbledegook, double-think and gudda." He said the official garda view was that I was probably not the mother of the Caherciveen baby yet the gardai asked to proceed in a prosecution. It would not even have been the basis for running a civil case, not to mention a criminal prosecution.

Mr O'Higgins had no time for gobbledegook.

Judge Lynch said that the internal garda inquiry would have

given ninety per cent immunity to our family. He asked why we had not stuck to our guns and told the two chief superintendents what had happened. Had the gardai a valid point in saying this was not reasonable?

Dermot McCarthy replied that our family's confidence in the gardai as a whole was so shaken that we were unwilling to go before any garda no matter what his rank or the colour of his uniform. He also pointed out that some gardai had refused to co-operate with the internal inquiry.

Each of the lawyers asked the judge to award full costs to their clients. That would be the easiest of the myriad questions the judge would have to address himself to in preparing his report to the Minister for Justice.

For us it was over at last, five months and a few days after it had begun in the bitterly cold first week of the year. It was warmer now but the bitterness remained.

How I wish that the Tribunal had never happened! Nothing will ever repair the damage done to us by those daily hearings, nor can anything restore my shattered faith and confidence in the forces of law and justice in this country. The newspaper headlines have created an image of me in the public mind, as if I was some kind of scarlet woman rather than the perhaps rather naive and inexperienced person I am. I have become the butt of obscene remarks and "jokes". In one disgusting instance a banner at the 1985 All-Ireland Football Final carried an utterly obscene and unfair reference to me, and a local publication, *Kerry's Eye,* added insult to injury by reproducing a photograph of the banner on its front page.

A woman from County Louth put the Tribunal in perspective when she wrote a letter to the *Irish Press:* "Who will even remember one of the gardai's names that the inquiry is supposed to be about in a few weeks' time? But no one will forget Joanne Hayes' name, and she had not done anything wrong according to the law."

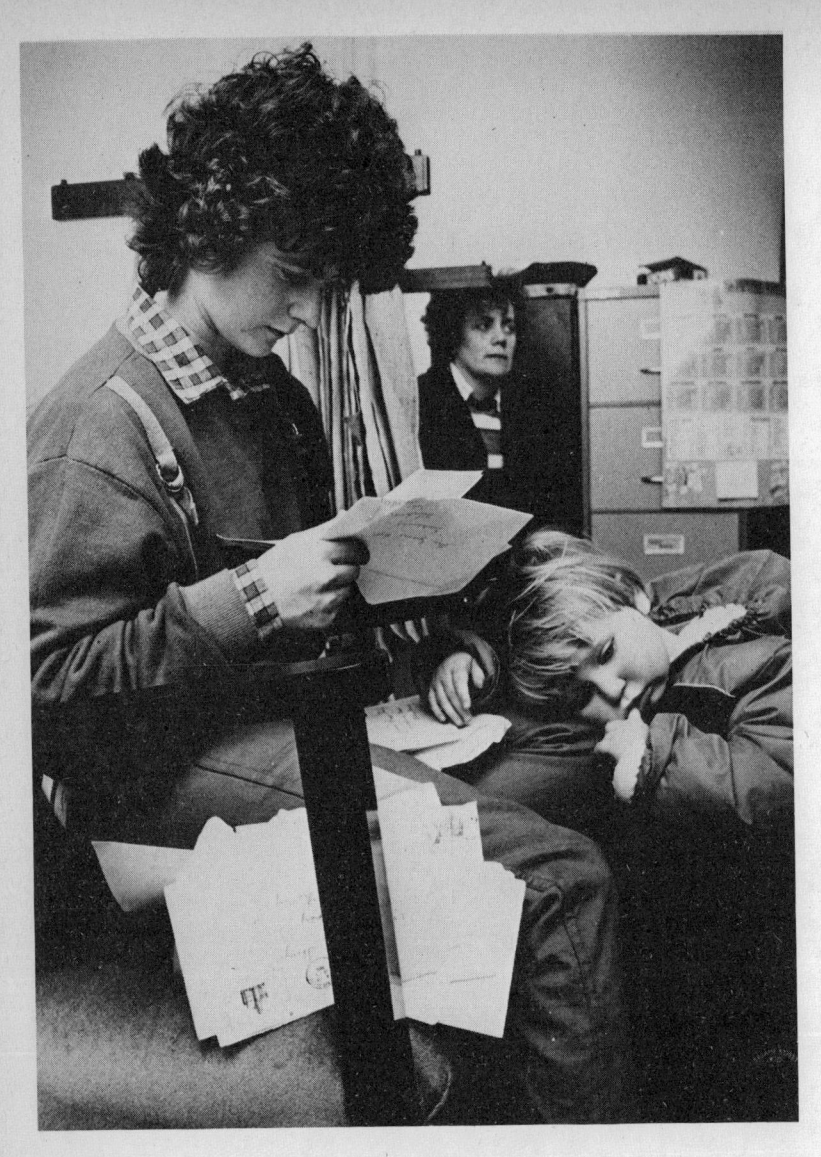

Reading letters of support, with Yvonne. (Michael MacSweeney).

Judge Lynch Reports

ON THURSDAY 3 October Judge Lynch published his report. It was made public with the same indifference to our feelings that we had experienced throughout our relations with the law in all its aspects: my hopes that I would be informed of the contents prior to its publication were shattered by a telephone call from a Dublin reporter. They were gathering to hear the awesome news.

Yvonne and I were visiting Helen O'Donovan, and Mom and Sister Aquinas had called on their way home from Edenburn Hospital where they had collected the last of Aunt Bridie's belongings. She had been spared this dreaded moment by a mere three days. Three friends were also present. The reporter had hinted that the judge had "come down hard" on me and the tension was unbearable as we waited for the five o'clock radio news bulletin.

The whispered prayers and aspirations were stilled as the judge's first lethal blow landed: I had killed my baby in my bedroom by putting my hands on its throat to stop it crying by choking it. I had also hit it with a bath brush in the presence of Mom and Kathleen.

My screams drowned the rest. Oh Jesus, not that, not after Dr Harbison's evidence. I became hysterical and heard no more. Would this never end? Dr Arthurs was called from Tralee and he arrived within minutes and treated me and talked to me for a long time. He was advising me about how to cope and how to face the days ahead. What days ahead? I had no future now, the label that had failed to stick just a year previously had been glued on this time with the imprimatur of a High Court judge.

Friends began calling and consoled me that he had found that I was not the mother of the Caherciveen baby, but that was no relief. I had always known that and so had the gardai if only they'd had the decency to admit it. Gradually the major findings emerged as later bulletins revealed that nothing that we had alleged about the gardai had been believed. We were all perjurers, apart from Aunt Bridie, and the lies that the gardai had told had been covered by euphemisms such as "gilding the lily".

171

Judge Lynch called it, "Report of the Tribunal of Inquiry into 'The Kerry Babies Case'," borrowing his title from a highly contentious journalistic phrase. We preferred to call it The Kerry Garda Case but, as the contents revealed, this was one book that could certainly be judged by its cover.

We were annihilated, individually and collectively, and discredited to an extent that even in our worst nightmares we could never have imagined. It had boiled down to a question of credibility and the gardai had triumphed apart from earning a slap or two for some slipshod work in their investigation and in their attitude towards the Twins Theory.

The judge relied heavily on Aunt Bridie's evidence. He said she was a truthful witness, but suggestible, and that her evidence had to be approached with caution. She would have been particularly vulnerable to suggestions that "she did that which ought to have been done". He accepted her evidence, and Mike's, that my baby was born in my bedroom despite the visible difficulties under which both she and Mike gave their evidence; and he rejected my true story, backed up by Doctor Louise McKenna and Doctor Creedon, that I had given birth outside.

He also chose Aunt Bridie's version that the baby had cried despite Doctor Harbison's evidence that he had failed to establish that my baby had achieved a separate existence and the discolouration on one side of the baby's throat could have been caused by the onset of decomposition. Dr Louise McKenna could find no evidence of a birth in my bedroom from the samples she analysed but she did say that vegetation found on my clothes were consistent with giving birth in a field. The judge disregarded the evidence of both of these state witnesses with regard to my baby. The judge's decision that Aunt Bridie cut the umbilical cord hurt me deeply because I would not have said that I had done so with my hands unless I knew it could be done. Dr Harbison had to conduct tests with medical students to prove that it was possible, but I knew from a year previously that it was possible because I had done it. To me this attitude of the judge to two state witnesses is the most hurtful of all, because it leads him to the conclusion that I killed my baby and that I beat it with a bathbrush. This really shattered me. Everything I suffered during the course of the Tribunal, everything else said about me in the report, pales into insignificance beside that.

I know that I and my family didn't acquit ourselves well in the witness box and that we didn't do ourselves justice, but that is for the very opposite reason that the judge has declared. He accused us in the report of having concocted a story, whereas in truth it was our failure to do so and to discuss the daily hearings of the Tribunal that got us into trouble through inconsistency and contradictions. If we had planned our strategy and lied to suit our case we would have done so much better. We couldn't have done any worse anyway because now Mom, Kathleen, Ned, Mike and I have been branded as perjurers by the learned judge. Poor Mom has been criticised in the report for what the judge called blatant perjury and being particularly "obsessed" with protecting and restoring the good name of the family.

The gardai planned their campaign but their good name is intact thanks to the judge who reported that their "agreed line of defence" was an example of the "familiarity breeds contempt" syndrome, which is a danger that the Oath may become for them largely a matter of form through having to give evidence in the course of their duty very frequently.

"They are not barefaced lies on the part of the gardai (as regrettably is the case with members of the Hayes family) but they are an exaggeration over and above the true position, or a gilding of the lily, or wishful thinking elevated to the status of hard fact," declared the judge. One of the examples he quoted was the persistence of the gardai in swearing that they were not questioning us about the Caherciveen baby and were simply trying to ascertain the facts about my pregnancy. They swore on that day after day before the judge and he admits that he finally lost patience with "the charade", as he termed it, but he would not call them liars. As far as I am concerned this attitude means that there was one set of standards for the gardai and a much tighter set for us. It is sickening.

Apparently Judge Lynch relied heavily on my expressions of guilt and remorse to Doctor Fennelly in Limerick — when he was treating me as "a very ill girl" — again despite the evidence of Doctor Harbison that he could not establish that my baby had achieved a separate existence. Even now I have very little recollection of my discussions with Doctor Fennelly, either in prison or in the hospital, and I think it unfair that I should be condemned on the strength of things which I said while under the influence of medication. And on the subject of my condition under interrogation and en route to prison it is remarkable that no reference is made about the various contradictory opinions expressed on Oath at the Tribunal, if only to decide whose version was correct.

While nailing me on my "disclosures" to the psychiatrist, Fennelly, the judge doesn't appear to accept the psychiatrist's assessment of Mike. He agreed that Mike was suggestible and asserted that "the female members of the Hayes family" had coached him for hours on end about what he should say in evidence; but then reported that "to suggest that he is so below normal and consequently so suggestible that little attention should be paid to what he said in evidence" would be a libel on Mike.

I don't wish to belittle Mike in any way and I have never for a second blamed him for anything he said in evidence, because I know that he was simply confused and totally overawed by the circumstances; but it is extremely annoying of Judge Lynch to decide that Mike's evidence that my baby was born in my bedroom came as a result of Mike's sudden grasping of the concept of the Oath. If Judge Lynch wanted to find out how well Mike had grasped the meaning of the Oath he should have asked him to explain it for him again ten minutes later. I have no doubt he would have been very surprised by Mike's answer.

At any rate, the Judge was satisfied to accept Mike's version and the evidence of Aunt Bridie, who didn't know what year this was or couldn't identify several old friends when they visited her, and largely on that base he feels justified in calling me a baby-killer.

None of us ever blamed Aunt Bridie for what proved such damning evidence because, to us, she was incapable of giving a coherent account of the events which she was asked to describe.

I visited her in hospital every Tuesday and Thursday, and brought Yvonne to see her, right up to two days before she died and I will never harbour any resentment against her. At her funeral people were saying that it was merciful that she had been taken from us before the report was published, but in fact the report would have meant nothing to her anyway.

That she should have been a central figure in all this is the supreme irony of the entire event, because she was deeply and genuinely loved by all of us. Tragically, she was totally misinterpreted by our most damaging adversaries when we most needed her.

To us the most inexplicable aspect of the judge's report came in his interpretation of our "confessions" under interrogation. He declared that it was the pressure of not knowing what had become of my baby and our guilty consciences with regard to the birth and death of the baby that led us to sign those "confessions". The vital question of how such identical detail was contained in "confessions" to a crime which we could not have committed is not posed or answered and the gardai are let off the hook. Those statements, written in what one eminent lawyer called "classic garda prose", included details about the non-existent trip to Slea Head and the knife used to stab the Caherciveen baby, but Judge Lynch has chosen not to provide the answers. If the Tribunal was supposed to resolve anything it was supposed to resolve that — the Terms of Reference make that absolutely clear. In my opinion, instead of doing what it was supposed to do the report explored every avenue which might be capable of making me look worse.

As the *Irish Times* editorial of 4 October said, the report "leaves a great many actions — principally those of the gardai — unexplained. . . . It fails to explain how the detailed statements from the Hayes family, tallying precisely in details which are now known to be false, came to be taken in Tralee Garda Station and at the Hayes farmhouse on May 1st and 2nd, 1984. Who came up with these details? How did they come to be translated into statements supposedly taken after caution?"

The Irish Times also points out that the report fails to decide whether we were in custody or not at Tralee Garda Station. The judge decided that he was satisfied that from the legal point of view none of us, including Jeremiah Locke, were arrested by the gardai for the purposes of being brought to Tralee Garda Station, but that the practical position was completely different because none of us appreciated our rights or our status as persons in the Garda Station. The judge also reports "the fact that Joanne Hayes was neither allowed to go out, nor taken out by the Gardai to show where her baby was on the lands, makes a mockery of the suggestion that she was a free agent, free to walk out of the Garda Station at any time she liked prior to about 8 p.m. The failure to bring Joanne Hayes out to the lands is the responsibility of Detective Superintendent Courtney." The judge adds that the reasons given by Detective Superintendent Courtney for not bringing me out to the farm were completely invalid.

For weeks on end the gardai swore that I and all the others were free to leave the station any time we wished. The judge found we were not, but he did not call the gardai liars, or perjurers or say they were obsessed with protecting and restoring the good name of the force.

The judge describes parts of the garda investigation as slipshod and says their failure to find my baby's body on the farm was inexcusable. The searches for my baby were deplorably inadequate, he said.

He was critical on the line of cross-examination of me on "a completely speculative basis as to other men with whom it was alleged that she might have had sexual intercourse at a time material to the events, the subject of the Tribunal's inquiry", and said he was satisfied that this cross-examination was conducted on the specific instructions of Detective Superintendent Courtney, who in his evidence expressed the view that I was a woman of "loose morals, which would suggest that she was accustomed to 'sleep around' indiscriminately, which is not true".

So, the judge decided that I was not promiscuous, but he was obviously distressed by the amount of support and sympathy which I received. "There are two women who have been far more gravely wronged than any wrong done to any member of the Hayes family," he reported. "Why no bouquets of flowers for Mrs Locke? Why no cards, no Mass Cards, for Mrs Locke? Why no public assemblies to support her in her embarrassment and agony?" All I can say is that Mrs Locke obviously wanted no publicity of any kind, and I just hope that she will be able to put all the unpleasantness behind her. The judge named Mrs Brigid Moloney, wife of Garda Liam Moloney, as the second gravely wronged woman and his remarks caused deep anger and resentment in Abbeydorney. He cited Garda Moloney's evidence that abusive telephone calls had been made to his wife and friends and said it was Abbeydorney people who made those calls. He said that as a result of the stress and unpleasantness imposed on her by these matters she lost a baby in the Summer of 1984 and he inferred that she was being made unwelcome in some shops. He said it painted a very clear picture of disgraceful and contemptible behaviour by some of the people of Abbeydorney and if he had known of these matters he would not have drawn the distinction between the Abbeydorney picket and the other picket when he issued his warnings against pickets on 28 January.

I doubt if anybody who took part in the Abbeydorney picket will lose any sleep over Judge Lynch's opinion of them, but there has been deep resentment at his allegations of the people's treatment of the Moloneys. His willingness to blame them for the loss of Mrs Moloney's baby, strictly on her husband's evidence and without any medical support, has angered many people, especially those who arranged for presentations and functions in honour of the Moloneys on their departure from the area. On the night before they left Ned shook hands with Garda Moloney and wished him luck and it was no secret that he was reluctant to leave.

Nobody would assert that Mrs Moloney was ever widely popular in Abbeydorney, even before these events started, but she had friends and it is impertinent to suggest that she was made unwelcome in the shops. Maybe the Moloneys will clear the air some day on that matter.

The report carried a neat point-by-point summary of the judge's conclusions and the media fastened on that immediately to broadcast the verdict to the nation. That night the television news bulletins churned out even more easily digestible summaries. On a *Today Tonight* current affairs' "special" a spokesperson for the gardai was visibly thrilled to take the opportunity to reiterate that the gardai had been exonerated.

The following morning the newspapers brought the verdict crashing down on us. The main item was that I had killed my baby; the fact that I was not the mother of the Caherciveen baby — as the gardai had alleged — was relegated to the margins. Again the emphasis was on the exoneration of the gardai. Page after page reproduced the judge's findings and the opinion makers rowed in behind him.

Mr Justice Lynch had done "a first class job" in producing "a splendid report". The *Irish Independent* was by far the worst. It paid tribute to the Tribunal's work, its "clear, hard-hitting report". Its front page screamed "Joanne's Shame" and its leader article heralded ". . . the destruction of a heroine". Beneath savage headlines — "How A Family Killed Truth" — the paper reproduced those parts of the report that damned us; power was triumphant. But magnanimous: its generosity was extended through the granting of our legal costs.

Other newspapers did print contrary opinions, such as that of the Council for the Status of Women, and the *Irish Times* put forward an informed and stinging criticism of the judge's findings. The evening papers too gave more critical opinion. In fact, as time wore on the pattern of the views began to change; sensationalism gave way to sobriety and obviously journalists and others had actually got around to reading the full report, not just the simple conclusions. Gradually the case was coming full circle, back to people's honest outrage at my inquisition.

The Tribunal had no such problem. The cold, unfeeling garda methods; the lawyers' clinical dissection of a living mind. The judge put his belief in men, accepting Jeremiah's rather cold version of our two-year relationship — our fling — and used it as a basis for further criticism of my part in our affair. I had, of course, been exposed already by the inquisition of my sexuality. Day after day the Tribunal had allowed every detail of my sex and my body to be exposed to limitless scrutiny. These lines of examination were likely to prove fruitless, the judge pointed to their lack of substance, the report showed their uselessness.

The way I see it now is that the law does not have any feeling or morality. The Rape Crisis Centre explains it better than I can when it said that the judge's comments "smack of the attitude that the Rape Crisis Centre has spent eight years trying to eradicate". "All along," the Centre continued, "women were brought up to believe that men have no power over their sexual urges, and that it is up to women to control them." But I had encouraged this "urge", lead it on, according to the judge. The judge's attitude to women and the problems heaped on their heads seems to be pretty don't-carish alright. "What is so unbelievably extraordinary about two women in County Kerry in one of the weeks in 1984, both deciding to do away with their babies?" he said in the report. Ah sure, maybe they just weren't "lawful" wives, "lawful" mothers, with "lawful" children.

Obviously this report has shattered my belief that I could pick up the threads again and get back to normal living and maybe a part-time job. We still have our friends and I know that Abbeydorney will never let us down, but I worry and feel guilty about the effects that this terrible business has had on Mom.

The rest of us are young enough to hope that time will heal the hurt and help us to forget what we have suffered. I will never forgive the people responsible, or believe in the concept of law and justice as I understood it.

It has been an unforgettable ordeal, but, as I keep reminding myself, I have Yvonne and she is worth it. Thank God for her.

Appendix: The Statements

Statement of Joanne Hayes:

I started to go out with Jermiah Locke who worked in the Sports Centre in Tralee with me as a groundsman. I knew he was married. Its exactly the 26th October, 1981 I first started to go out with him. He told me that he wasn't getting on with his wife. I fell deeply in love with him, and we were very intimate from the very beginning. Around May, 1982 I became pregnant by Jermiah but around the Bank-Holiday in June I think it was the Sunday I lost the baby. I wanted to be pregnant. I thought from the beginning that Jermiah Locke would go away with me and that we would live together happily ever after. I remained going out with Jermiah and on the 19th May, 1983 I had a baby girl in St. Catherine Hospital in Tralee. I called the baby Yvonne. I still thought that Jermiah would go away with me especially after having the baby for him. Jermiah only saw Yvonne twice and that also upset me. I stayed going out with Jermiah and I still loved him and he said he loved me and that he might go away with me eventually. I became pregnant again for him last year and I had my last period in August, 1983. My mother and all the lads at home were upset about the first baby, but they accepted it and they decided to help me to rear it. They were all very upset when I became pregnant again and I was thoroughly and absolutely ashamed of myself and I tried to hide it. I wore tight clothes and I tried not to let it show. On the 12th/13th April, 1984 I was at home in the farmhouse in my own room, the baby Yvonne was in the cot. Sometime during the night I started to go into Labour and a baby boy was born. I was in my own bed in my own room in the old farmhouse. My Auntie Bridie Fuller was present at the birth and delivered the baby. Michael my brother was in the house at the time. The baby was alive and crying and my Auntie Bridie placed him at the end of the bed. She left the room to make a pot of tea and I got up and went to the toilet. On the way back to the bedroom I picked up the white Bath Brush and I went to the cabinet in the kitchen and picked up the Carving knife with the brown timber handle. These are the items i.e. the White Bath Brush and the Brown Timber-handled carving knife. I have been shown here today by Detective Garda Smith and Coote. I went back to the bedroom and I hit the baby on the head with the Bath Brush. I had to kill him because of the shame it was going to bring on the family and because Jeremiah Locke would not run away and live with me. The baby cried when I hit it and I stabbed it with the carving knife on the chest and all over the body. I turned the baby over and I also stabbed him in the back. The baby stopped crying after I stabbed it. There was blood everywhere on the bed and there was also blood on the floor.

I then threw the knife on the floor. My Mother, Auntie Bridie, Kathleen my sister and my two brothers Ned and Mike ran into the bedroom. I was crying and so was my Mother, my sister Kathleen and my Auntie Bridie. I told them I would have to get rid of the body of the baby and then my two brothers said they would bury it. I told them to take away the baby from the farmyard and they said they would. Everyone was panicking at this stage. The boys then brought in a white plastic bag and they put the baby into it and then they put this bag into a turf bag similiar to the one Detectives Smith and Coote showed me earlier on this evening at the Station. The boys then left in our own car with the baby. I heard the car leaving the back-yard. I was feeling sick and depressed and upset, soon afterwards the afterbirth came and I put into a brown bucket beside the bed. I then changed the sheets and I put the bloody sheets on the floor until the following day. I then took my baby Yvonne into my bed and Bridie remained on in the house, all the others left and went to our cottage about a hundred yards away. I got up around 5am and I took the brown bucket with the afterbirth in it and I went out the front and I put the afterbirth into the old hay beside the well. I went back up to the house and I went to bed again. I woke up again at about 7.30am and my brother Michael was back in the house again. I started to clear up my bedroom after that. I gathered up all the sheets that had blood on them and the brown handled carving knife and the white bath brush. I washed the knife and the brush and put them back in their proper places. I then washed the sheets. All day Friday I was bleeding heavily and feeling bad and my sister Kathleen went up for two neighbours, a Mrs. Mary Shanahan and Elsie Moore who is a Nurse. I was then taken to Doctor Dalys Surgery in Elsie Moores car along with Mrs. Mary Shanahan. I told the two neighbours that I had a miscarraige. I told Doctor Daly I had a miscarraige. Dr. Daly examined me and told me that I hadn't lost the child and that I was four months pregnant. He gave me a letter for St. Catherines Hospital, Tralee to go in as soon as possible. I didn't go into hospital that night as I did not want to leave Yvonne. On the next day Saturday the 14th April, 1984 my brother Ned took me into St. Catherines Hospital. I was examined by a doctor, a lady doctor, a tall very thin lady with black hair. This lady doctor told me after examining me that I was pregnant. She didn't say for how long. I had told her I thought I had a miscarriage. I was kept in the hospital until the following Saturday, when I was discharged. Since the night that I killed my baby there was never any talk about it in the house. When the body of the baby was found at Caherciveen I know deep-down it was my baby. I was going to call him Shane. I am awful sorry for what happened, may God forgive me. I have heard this statement read over to me and it is correct. I dont want to change any of it.

Statement of Kathleen Hayes:

I reside at Droumcunnig, Abbeydorney on my mothers farm of about sixty acres. My widowed mother, my Aunt Bridie who is a retired nurse, who is my mothers sister, my two brothers Ned 27 years and Mike who is 26 years and my sister Joanne 25 years and her baby daughter Yvonne. I remember Thursday night 12th of April, 1984, I was sleeping in the same bedroom as my sister Joanne and her daughter Yvonne. Joanne was sleeping in her own bed, Yvonne was in her cot and I was sleeping on a mattress on the floor. At about 12 mid-night on Thursday 12th April, 1984 I returned home after being visiting Tony Lyon's house who is a neighbour of ours. When I came in home my mother and my brother Mike were in the kitchen. Joanne was in her bedroom with Yvonne. My Aunt Bridie was also in bed. I went to Joannes room and she asked me to change Yvonne's nappy and get her ready for bed. Joanne was standing beside the bed and Yvonne was down on the bed. I asked my brother Mike who was standing at the door of Joanne's bedroom to hold the baby for a few minutes while I was getting her clothes in the kitchen. When I returned with the babys clothes, Mike went to bed, the bedroom is next to Joanne's. My mother went to bed. Almost immediately after Mike and Joanne went out the front door, she told me I am better off out in the fresh air I'm walking around all night. I knew she was pregnant but I thought she was about seven months pregnant. When I had finished getting Yvonne ready for bed I put her into Joannes bed. I then went out the front door at about 12.30am on Friday 13th April, 1984. I called Joanne, the light outside the front door was on I could not see her, but she answered my call, she said I am alright I'll be in, in a minute. She came in at about 1.15am and at this time I was lying inside on Joannes bed with Yvonne. I heard Joanne in the kitchen and then I heard her going to the bathroom and locking the door of the bathroom. After about a quarter of an hour she came out of the bathroom. I had gone from the bedroom to the kitchen and I was talking to Joanne for a minute in the kitchen. She went to bed before me. When she had left the kitchen I saw drops of blood on the kitchen floor near the hot press. I then went to Joanne's bedroom. She said to me "I had a heavy period and asked me for some towels". I told her I had none. It was about 1.45am at this time. I lay down on the mattress on the floor and Joanne was in bed and Yvonne was inside her in the bed. At about 2am on 13th/4/'84 Joanne called me and asked me if I was asleep, I answered her, she said "I think I am having a baby". I got up and I called my Aunt Bridie who came up to Joanne's bedroom. Bridie then called Mom. My brother Mike who is sleeping in the same room as Mom also got up. I took Yvonne from Joanne's bed and put her into her cot. She was asleep when I put her into her cot. Joanne was having labour pains and Aunt Bridie went to assist Joanne in having the baby. My Mother and brother Mike were present in the room when the baby was born. The baby was crying after birth. It was a baby boy. Joanne was upset when the baby was born and she was crying. I said "the baby was a fine little lad". My Aunt Bridie cut the umbylical cord with a scissors. She placed the baby at the end of the bed on the bed clothes. I went to the kitchen and got a basin of luke warm water and gave it to my Aunt Bridie. She washed the baby and washed Joanne. There was blood on the sheets in the bed. My Mother, my brother Mike was also present when the baby was born. My mother was upset and she said "one of his children was enough to have" meaning Jeremiah Locke from Shanakill, Monavalley, Tralee. We all knew he was the father as he was the father of her first child, Yvonne who will be one year old on 19th May, 1984, he is a married man. I took the basin of water down to the kitchen and when I returned Aunt Bridie was gone to her room and my mother and Mike were in the room with Joanne and the new baby. Joanne was crying and was crouched over the baby in the bed in a kneeling position and she was chocking the baby with her two hands. She was shaking all over when she was doing this and the baby was screaching while she was choking it. No one tried to stop her from doing this to the baby. Joanne asked me to go down to the kitchen to get the carving knife from the drawer in the cabinet. I got the knife for her and I handed her the knife. Joanne then stabbed the baby with the point of the carving knife in the chest about six or seven times. She was in a temper when she was stabbing the baby. I have been shown a carving knife "Prestige" make by D/Gda. Smith and I now identify the knife to Garda Moloney and D/Gda. Smith as being the knife that I handed to my sister Joanne when she stabbed the baby in the bedroom on Friday morning 13th April, 1984 at approximately 2.45a.m. My mother, my brother Mike and my Aunt Bridie and myself were present in the room when Joanne was stabbing the baby with the carving knife. The baby died from the chocking and the stabbing and it was dead when my mother and I left the room to go up to our other house which is about 150 yards away from my house to call my brother Ned who is sleeping there. It was 3am when we went to call Ned. It was dark and I was using a flash lamp to give us light on the way up. We knocked up Ned and I told Ned to come down Joanne had a baby and that the baby was dead. Ned hopped out of bed and came down to our own house after us. He went to Joannes room and he saw the dead baby with stab wounds on Joannes bed. Joanne was in the kitchen when Ned came to the house. After Ned had seen the baby he was very upset. He said "why did you killl the baby". We were all upset at that stage and we didn't know what to do. We thought we might bury it on the farm. Mike said will we bury it back the field but Mom and Aunt Bridie were against that. So then we decided we will have to dump it some where. Mike when to the back kitchen to get a turf bag and I went to a drawer under the Television and got a white plastic bag with two handles, like the ordinary shopping bag you would get in Supermarkets. I held the white plastic bag and Ned put the dead baby into it. We done this in the bedroom and then Ned put the white plastic bag containing the baby into a turf bag which Mike had got in the back kitchen. I have been shown a bag by D/Garda Smith and I believe that it was a bag of similar colour and material as the bag in which the white plastic bag containing the baby was put into. The bag containing the baby was then brought out to the back kitchen, by Ned and Mike tied the bag with a piece of twine. Ned then took out the bag and put it into the booth of our car. Ned, Mike and I left our house at about 3.50am in our car a Blue Ford Fiesta Reg. No. 822-ZX we drove through Tralee on through Dingle town for about six miles and we stopped at a place where the road runs beside the sea, and Ned who was driving got out and opened the booth of the car and took out the bag containing the baby and threw it into the sea. It was about 5.30am on Friday 13th April, 1984, when Ned threw the bag into the sea. You could see the water from the road where we were parked and when the bag was thrown in, it sank, and re-surfaced and floated on the water. We arrived back home at 7am. Ned drove the car that morning when we were disposing of the baby I was in the front passenger seat, and Mike was sitting in the back seat. We told my Mother, Joanne and Bridie that we had thrown the baby into the sea back around Dingle. At 9.30pm on Friday 13th April, 1984 Mary Shanahan and Elsie Moore more neighbours of ours brought Joanne to Dr. Daly, Tralee as I called to them to tell them that Joanne was very pale and lossed a lot of blood. So Elsie Moore who is a district Nurse said she would take her to a doctor. When she had been to the Doctor, Dr. Daly said she would have to go to Hospital that night. But she refused to go that night. He said she would have to go to Hospital for a check-up the next day. So Ned took her to St. Catherines Hospital, Tralee on Saturday 14th April, 1984. She was in Hospital for one week and was discharged from St. Catherines Hospital on 21st April, 1984. She had to get two pints of blood while she was in Hospital. I went to visit her every day she was in Hospital. This statement has been read over to me by D/Garda Smith and I have been invited to make any changes or alterations, but I do not wish to make any changes as it is correct.

Statement of Edmund (Ned) Hayes:

I reside at the above address with my Mother, Mary Hayes and my sister Kathleen in a cottage. In the nearby farmhouse my Aunt Bridie Fuller, a retired nurse, my brother Michael 26 years who runs the farm and sister Joanne 25 years and her year old child reside. My sister Joanne works in the Tralee Sports Complex. She has been going out with a Jeremiah Locke, who is a married man for the past two years. I know him to be the father of my sisters child Yvonne. My sister Joanne was out of work for about 23 weeks on maternity leave when Yvonne was born. About three months ago I learned from my mother that Joanne was pregnant again. I was surprised to learn this as I thought the affair with Locke was over. I can remember Thursday morning 12th April, 1984. I got up around 10am I was alone in the cottage for sleeping purposes the night before as my mother had an awful dose of the flu. When I came down my mother was sitting at one side of the fire, my Aunt Bridie was on the other, Yvonne was sitting on her chair and Joanne was getting the breakfast. Kathleen and Michael were finishing the milking of the cows outside. Around 10.15am — 10.30am we all had breakfast together. A Brendan Fitzmaurice, Boonreigh, Abbeydorney called about 10.30am as he had been putting in windows and doors in the cottage for about three weeks. Around 10.45am I went to Abbeydorney and got some messages (litre milk, nappies and the paper) from Donovans and Shanahans. I was back around 11am, Brendan Fitzmaurice was gone up to the cottage so I went up after him. Around 1pm my sister Kathleen called us to the dinner. We all had dinner except Joanne, who I heard telling my mother that she wasn't having dinner that she had a pain in her stomach and that she was going to bed when we had eaten. After dinner Joanne called me up into the room and asked me to ring my Auntie Joan Fuller in Newbridge Parochial House and my Auntie Sister Acquinas in Ballybunion and Liam Bohane personally in Tralee Sports Centre. I had to tell all three that she had a pain in her stomach and that she wouldn't be at work that day. I asked Michael to go up with Brendan while I went to Abbeydorney. I left the house around 1.30pm. I met Kevin Roche, Glounametig, Abbeydorney on the way and asked to use his phone for a long distance call. I made the phone call to Newbridge from Kevin Roches house where I met his wife Maureen. I rang Sister Acquinas from the "Silver Dollar", Abbeydorney. Both my aunts were out but I left messages for them. After about a half an hour I made contact with Liam Bohane. I came home around 2.45pm. I told my mother that I had made the phone calls and I went up to the cottage to Brendan were we were working until about 6pm. I stayed cleaning floors until about 7pm. on my own. I went down to the farmhouse about that time and had supper with the rest of the family with the exception of Joanne and Auntie Bridie who was in bed. After supper, I went in the car down to Kevin Roches for a talk about the hurling and football teams. Before I went to Kevin Roches I went to Maurice Roches where I got £10 worth of petrol. Around 9.30pm I left Kevin Roches and went to the "Silver Dollar" pub. Bill Behan, Stevie Glavin and Ned Mc Elligott were playing cards there. I drank alone and had a half whiskey and four pints. I went home about 11pm. I left the keys of the car in the farmhouse on top of the television. My mother was alone in the kitchen when I got back. I went back up to the cottage alone for the night. I went to bed straight away after going home and I was reading a book called "The Great Hunger" until about 12M.N. I turned off the light and fell asleep. Sometime during the night around 2.30am I would think, I was awakened to my sister Kathleen knocking on the front room window where I sleep. She asked me to come down quick. She sounded excited and she left. I got up, had a drink of water and went down to the farmhouse after about 15 minutes. I met my mother walking out the boreen outside the house to meet me. She said that we had big trouble here at the moment. She told me that Joanne was after having a child and that she, Joanne was after doing away with the child. She was crying and looked very upset. We went into the kitchen and my brother and sister Kathleen were inside. The two of them were balling crying and they were very upset. I was shattered and I was shaking all over. I sat on a chair beside the table with my back to all the bedrooms. I took a drink of orange to try to cool my nerves. I went up into Joannes room. I met my Auntie Bridie just coming out of the room. She was crying and shaking all over. I stood at the door of the room. I saw Joanne lying on the bed with just a night dress on. I saw the body of a newly born child at the foot of the bed. I have drawn a sketch of the room and what I saw when I went into the room. The infant was lying face downwards naked on the bed. I said to my sister "what in fucks name did you do it" I said to her that surely we could have kept the child and reared it. She did not answer as she was crying away. I went away from the door and went back up a couple of minutes afterwards. I repeated what I said the first time and she said that she didn't want to bring shame on the family. She said that six months ago Locke said that they would go away together and set up house. I went back down to the kitchen where there was a cup of tea ready. We all had tea. There wasn't a word spoken about it. I went out for a breath of fresh air for about 10 minutes and when I came back in, my mother suggested that we would have to get some way of getting rid of it. We talked for about three quarters of an hour of getting rid of it. I was in favour of burying it on the land but my mother and Auntie Bridie weren't in favour of it. Auntie Bridie was in favour of us throwing it in the sea. My brother and I went outside to get a plastic bag. My brother picked up a fertilizer bag from the gable end of the house. I shone a torch for him to find it. The bag had some sand in it for putting on top of sileage. He emptied out the sand. We went into the kitchen and up into Joannes room. I emptied out a brown plastic shopping bag of clothes which I found beside the wardrobe in the room. We caught a leg each of the infant and put it head first into the brown shopping bag. As we lifted the dead infant I could see blood on its chest. It was stabbed in the chest, I couldn't say how may wounds were in the chest. When we had placed the dead infant in the brown plastic bag. Joanne asked to be left alone in the room with the child for a few minutes. Both of usm went back to the kitchen and left her alone for about 10 minutes. We layed the bag containing the infant on the floor beside the bed. When we returned to the room, she was on the bed turned towards the wall. The brown bag had been rolled closed so that the infant was not visible. We opened the grey fertilizer bag which was an 0-7.-30, wider and each caught an end of the brown bag and put it into the grey bag. I have on this date been shown a grey fertilizer bag 0.-7-30 and a brown shopping bag by D/Sgt. Dillon and they are similar to the ones we use that morning. When we had placed the brown bag with the infant into the grey bag, my sister Joanne asked to be left alone again with the infant. We again placed it on the floor and left for about 2 minutes. When we returned she was in a similar position facing the wall and the top of the grey bag was tied with a string. I caught hold of the top of the bag and Michael caught the bottom of the bag. We took it through the kitchen. My sister Kathleen had the door of the car open as I had already asked her. Kathleen had the keys of the car and she handed me the keys of the car afterwards. I placed the bag on the floor of the car behind the drivers seat. Our car is a Ford Fiesta, blue colour registered number 822-ZX. The car is the property of my Auntie Bridie but both Michael and myself are insured to drive it. I went back into the house and brought a road map with me. I went back into the kitchen and told my mother and Aunt that we were leaving. My sister Kathleen had gone down into Joannes room where she was sleeping on a mattress. I drove the car and my brother accompanied me in the front passenger seat of the car which is a two door. We brought a shovel with us in case we might get a quite place to bury it. We had fully intended when we left the house that we would go to the sea with the bag and the further away the better. I drove the car into Tralee onto Blennerville, out the Dingle Road. At Camp Cross I stopped and took out the map to decide which road we would go. We decided to go by Conor Pass as we thought it would be quietest. Going up Conor Pass we stopped for about 3 minutes and looked at the map again to decide which way we would go. We didn't pick out any place on the map to dispose of the body and we decided to drive on for another bit. We went on into Dingle and went out the Ventry Road. We stopped this side of Ventry and looked at the map again. It was then we decided to go to Slea Head. We drove on until we came to a spot about 2 miles on the Ventry side of Slea Head. I am familiar with Ventry and Slea Head as I have been there on a number of occasions. When I got to this spot which I thought was the most suitable place I got out of the car and took out the bag containing the body. I walked around the back of the car with the bag and opened the door for my brother. I asked my brother to keep a watch out and I went in over a stone ditch, walked about 20 yards to the edge of the cliff. I flung the bag from the cliff and into the sea. I would say there was a drop of about 10 feet and I watched the bag drop directly into the water. I returned to the car, turned the car about on the roadway and drove back the same way as we had come. We arrived back home in Abbeydorney about 10am. . . . I feel much better now that I have told you the truth. This statement has been read over to me and I have been asked to make any alterations and additions, and it is correct. I have made the statement freely and voluntarily.

Statement of Michael Hayes:

I reside in the home farmhouse with my Aunt Bridie Fuller and my sister Johanna Hayes. My mother and my brother Ned and sister Kathleen live in a council cottage next door on the Tralee side. My sister Johanna works at the Sports Centre, Tralee in the office for the last 2 to 3 years. She is single and about 24 yrs About one and a half years ago she gave birth to a baby girl. It was born at St. Catherines Hospital, Tralee. She kept the child at home and my mother Mary and Aunt looked after it while she was at work. Kathleen my sister also looked after the child in her absence. The childs name is Siobhan Hayes. I knew the father because he called to our house before the child was born and Johanna told me he worked at the Sports Centre where she worked. The family were saying it in the house that he was a married man. I thought it was an awful thing to happen, he being a married man. Sometime after Christmas 1983 I could see that Johanna was pregnant again. She was getting big. I didn't ask her if she was pregnant but it was talked about by the family. I was worried that she was meeting the same fellow and that she was pregnant after him but I dont know who the father is. The first time she was pregnant she was seeing Doctor Hayes, Tralee but I dont think she was seeing any doctor this time. She used to go to work and I dont know if she was going to work or not. About 2 weeks before Easter, 1984 she was at home on holidays and she was on sick leave as well. On the Tuesday night of the week before Easter week myself Johanna and Bridie, my Aunt went to bed at about 11.30pm to three different rooms. Shortly after going to bed I went to sleep. I was awakened at about 2am to 2.30am by a person roaring and shouting. I got up and I heard that the shouting and roaring was coming from Johanna's room. I went into her room, my Aunt was there before me standing near the top of Johanna's bed. Siobhan was in a cot beside the side of the bed. There was a new born baby on the bed beside Johanna and she had her arm around it. The bedspread was wrapped around the baby. The baby was alive and crying. I got a fright when I saw another baby there again eventhough I knew she was expecting. I was frightened all the time, when she wasn't married or anything. I stayed for a few minutes in the room, I didn't say anything. My Aunt was saying something, I don't know what she said. I left my Aunt in the room and went out to the kitchen. My sister Kathleen who had stayed in the same room as Johanna was also in the room. My mother who had slept in the room with me had gone into Johanna's room before me, and she was also in the room. I had put on my clothes before leaving my bedroom. My mother, Aunt and sister Kathleen were giving out to her for having this child and going out with a married man. They were cross with her. I was up and down to the room every couple of minutes. I did this a lot of times. My mother, Aunt and Kathleen were in the room all this time. My mother left the room and went to the kitchen. Kathleen then brought up a toilet brush from the bathroom, to the bedroom. She gave the brush to Johanna. I was standing at the door, Kathleen went into the kitchen and got a kitchen knife from a cabinet in the kitchen inside the back door. It was a pointed knife, it had a rough blade and brown timber handle and she gave it to Johanna who was inside in bed. The baby was beside Johanna in the bed. Johanna stabbed the baby on the chest three times. The bedspread was all blood after. The baby's face was towards the ceiling and its feet were facing the bottom of the bed. I stayed standing, Kathleen was near the bed when Johanna was doing it, my Aunt was also in the room near the bed at this time. Then Johanna got out of bed. I saw her catch hold of the toilet brush in her right hand and she hit the child in the face and body a number of times. The baby was on the floor at this stage as it had fallen off the bed when Johanna was getting out of bed. Johanna put the baby up on the bed then. The bedspread was still around the baby. The baby was dead at this stage. My mother came into the room. Ned my brother came into the bedroom at this stage. My mother said that we'd bury the body in the field, the rest of us said we would throw it into the sea. Myself and Ned went out to the back yard. We got blue manure bag similar to the one shown to me to-day by D/Garda John O'Sullivan. We got a big stone in the yard which we dug up, and we put it into the bag. I stayed in the yard and Ned went into the house. I then went up to the back door. The light was on in the back kitchen. Ned came out to the back kitchen with Kathleen they had the baby rapped up in a newspaper and a clear plastic bag and a brown shopping bag similar to the two bags shown to me by D/Gda. J. Sullivan. I hold the manure bag and Ned put the baby's body which I saw was a baby boy into the manure bag. I got a piece of binder twine off a bale of hay in the shed and tied the top of the bag down about half ways. Ned put it into the booth of our Ford Fiesta car. Ned drove the car and I sat in the front passenger seat. We didn't know where we would go at that time. It was about 4.30am Wednesday morning we drove into Tralee. We went down by the Dingle Bridge outside Tralee. We stopped after passing the bridge and Ned took out a map. We decided to drive down to Dingle. We went over the mountain road. We went through one village on the way and when we got into Dingle we turned right and we continued, straight on until we came to a bridge about a mile from the town. We continued straight on for about 7 or 8 miles. We were near the sea then and Ned took the bag with the body in it and he crossed over a field and I saw him throwing the bag containing the baby's body into the sea. The sun was just rising in the sky then. I had no watch on me and I don't know what time. We came back to Tralee by the same road. We got petrol in Tralee at Horans Garage. We drove home then. I had my breakfast and milked the cows and went to the creamery. We tried to keep it all quite and it looks like we didn't succeed. I have heard this statement read over to me by D/Garda John O'Sullivan, I have been asked to make any alterations or additions I deem necessary. It is correct and true.

Statement of Bridie Fuller:

I was born on the 20/11/1915. I am telling the truth about what happened to my niece Joanne the night her last baby was born in April of this year. I know Joanne was pregnant by Jeremiah Locke from Tralee, but I couldn't say for certain how far she was gone.

Joanne was living at the time in the farmhouse with her brother, Michael, and her daughter Yvonne, who is nearly a year old. I went to bed that evening early as I usually wake at about 12 or so. I must have been awake about one and Michael was up also. I went down to Joanne's room and she was getting in and out of bed. I suspected that she was after going into labour. I sent Michael up to the cottage where my sister Mary and her daughter Kathleen and son Ned were living.

Kathleen and Mary came down to our house and I told them that Joanne was in labour. Someone else went for Ned. I am scattered about that. I think it was Michael. It was now 2.30 and Joanne was at an advanced stage. We went up to see her and I helped break her waters. The baby was then born and I did the best I could to help her. It was a baby boy. I saw it move and I saw it was bubbling with mucus. I was not in the room when the baby died. I think I made tea in the kitchen.

After this I don't know what happened, but I remember that it was light before I got back to bed. I stayed in bed for a while and Michael milked the cows around 7 o'clock that morning. Joanne was above in the bed and Michael went to the creamery. Kathleen came down while they were milking to the farmhouse. Joanne got up late and I don't know what happened to the baby.

Joanne went into hospital on Saturday after seeing the doctor. She had to go to the hospital with Ned and she got two units of blood. She was there until Easter Saturday when she came home. She went back to work two days ago at the Sports Complex in Tralee.

She told me tonight that she had killed the baby the night it was born and I am so bothered by it all that I can't say any more. This statement has been read over to me and it is correct.''

Statement of Mrs Mary Hayes, 5 p.m., 1 May:

I reside at the above address with my children Kathleen D.O.B. 16/12/1954, Edward D.O.B. 20/1/1956, Michael D.O.B. 24/1/1957, Joanne D.O.B. 30/4/1959. We run a sixty acre farm. On the 19/5/1983 my daughter Joanne had a baby daughter in St. Catherines Hospital, Tralee. The father of the child is Jeremiah Locke of Tralee and he is a married man. Joanne met him after getting a job at the Sports Complex, Tralee. Joanne works at the Reception and Jeremiah works as a Groundsman. On or about the 7th April, 1984 I got the flu and spent most of my time in bed until Easter week. I remember Friday 15/4/1984 around 3 p.m. I saw drops of blood on the kitchen floor and I asked Joanne what was that on the floor and she Joanne told me that she was having a heavy period and that she was not feeling well and she was going to see her Doctor who is Dr. Daly, Tralee. She, Joanne spent most of the day going in and out of the toilet. At about 9.30 p.m. on Friday 15/4/1984 Nurse Elsie Moore living at Shanahans, Listellig, Tralee, took Joanne to Dr. Daly. My daughter Kathleen went to Shanahans to get Nurse Moore. Dr. Daly gave Joanne a letter for to go to Hospital that eveing but she said she would wait until the following morning. The following morning Saturday 16/4/1984 at 10 a.m. approx. Joanne got up out of bed and got ready to go to the Hospital. My son Ned drove her at about 10.30 a.m. because she had to be at the Hospital for 11 a.m. She returned home on Saturday 23/4/1984 at about 12 m.d. On Easter Sunday my sister who is a nun in Ballybunion Sr. Acquinas told me that Joanne had a miscarriage, three months. I never asked Joanne about the miscarriage but just asked her if she was alright. I have heard this statement read over to me and it is correct.

189

Second Statement of Mrs Mary Hayes, 6-7 p.m., 1 May:

I remember Tuesday night 10th April, 1984 at 7 p.m. I knew Joanne my daughter was ill as she was loosing alot of blood around and I knew she was about to have a baby. In the house with me was my sister Bridie Fuller who is a retired Nurse, who lives with me, my son Mike and daughter Kathleen. At about 2.30 a.m. the following morning 11/4/1984 Joanne had a baby down in her own room. Bridie, Mike and Kathleen was with her. After the child was born Mike and Kathleen came down from Joannes room to tell me in the kitchen about the birth of the child and they left Bridie alone with Joanne. About five minutes later Bridie came down to the kitchen to tell me to go down quick and see the child and Joanne, Kathleen and Mike came with me and in the bedroom I saw Joanne lying in her bed and the baby was at the bottom of the bed. I saw that the baby was dead and its body was marked, I saw a white toilet brush beside the bed and Joanne used that brush to beat the child. I then left with Kathleen to call my other son Ned who was in bed above in our other house which is about 100 yards away. Before I left to go up for Ned Joanne was crying out aloud and was very upset. I saw her with the toilet brush in her hand. When I arrived back down with Ned Joanne had calmed back down. I said to Joanne "you will have to bury the child" and Mike or Kathleen said we will bury the child on the land. I said the child cannot be buried on the land. Ned and Mike went to the back kitchen where they got a turf bag and put the child into the bag. I told mike and Ned that they would have to bury the child. They left Mike and Ned with the child in the bag and drove out of the yard at about 5 a.m. They Mike and Ned returned at about 7 a.m. and said that they had buried the child. I did not ask them where. We all decided not to talk or tell anybody about it. On Friday 13/4/1984 Joanne was still loosing blood and Kathleen got Nurse Elsie Moore to take her to Dr. Daly. Dr. Daly ordered her to go to hospital and the following day Ned drove her to the Hospital at 11 a.m. that was Saturday 14/4/1984. My sister who is a Nun in Ballybunion Sr. Aquinas told me that Joanne was after a miscarriage of three months and Bridie told her of the birth. Joanne's room was all blood after the birth and when Joanne got up the following day she washed the bed clothes and room. We know who the father of the child was, Jeremiah Locke of Tralee and he is the father of her other child Yvonne who was born on 19/5/1983. Locke is a married man. I live with Ned and Kathleen in the new house and Bridie, Mike and Joanne live in the old house but we all eat our meals in the old house. I have been shown the white toilet brush by D/Garda Smith and I identified it as the brush Joanne had with her the night the child was born. I have also been shown a turf bag by D/Gda. Smith and that is similar to the one used by Mike and Ned to take away the baby. I have shown a carving knife by D/Garda Smith and that is the knife we normally carve the meat with. My husband died on 25/8/1975 and I have brought up my children with the help of my sister Bridie Fuller who has lived with me all her life. I have heard this statement read over to me and it is correct.

Popular Reading from Brandon

John B. Keane: *Man of the Triple Name* and *Owl Sandwiches*

John B. Keane's wonderful book about the last of the great Irish matchmakers, *Man of the Triple Name,* is "old-style storytelling at its best" *(Irish Post),* "hilarious social history" *(Boston Irish News)* and "hugely enjoyable" *(In Dublin).*

Owl Sandwiches is John B. at his most humorous and popular, and it is marked by "wit and vivacity, and darn good entertainment by a master craftsman" *(Derry Journal).* It is, as *Ireland's Own* put it, a "happy collection" of stories.

Leland Bardwell: *The House*

A novel about a house, a family and love, it is a positive gem; it shines with a lustre that glints not only in the mind but in the heart and soul as well". *(Sunday Press)*

Dermot Bolger: *Night Shift*

"No Irish novelist since McGahern has been so obsessed with the poetics of love, death and sex. No Irish novelist has so brilliantly captured the suburban underbelly of the city, the crazy unofficial lives."

Tony Cafferky: *Baulox*

In this hilarious novel "Tony Cafferky has constructed with great skill and flair a brave new world of the late 20th century." *(In Dublin)*

Philip Davison: *Twist and Shout*

Rock musician "Terry Hatchel and his friends are as much a part of Irish urban culture today, with their casual attitude to drugs and sex and their indifference to the Church and to the norms of middle class suburbia, as Edna O'Brien's country girls were to the world of repressed sexuality and drab conformity in the early 1960s." *(In Dublin)*

Pauline Hall: *Grounds*

A wonderful story of an Irish girl growing into womanhood in Dublin, France and the United States.

Steve Matheson: *Maurice Walsh, Storyteller*

The first biography of this immensely popular writer, author of "The Quiet Man" and books such as *The Key Above the Door* and *Blackcock's Feather*.

Anthony Cronin: *An Irish Eye* and *Heritage Now*

In *An Irish Eye* one of Ireland's most prominent authors explores what it means to be Irish. "This book establishes Cronin's contribution as central to the great debate on reality and society in Ireland." *(Magill)*

And in *Heritage Now* he offers a lively and engaging study of Irish literature in the English language. As Anthony Burgess has written, "Anthony Cronin's reading is wide, his insights astonishing."